Colleges *for* Freedom

A Study of
Purposes, Practices and Needs

DONALD J. COWLING
President of Carleton College, 1909–1945

CARTER DAVIDSON
President of Knox College, 1936–1946
and of Union College since 1946

HARPER & BROTHERS
New York, London

Dedicated to

Preface

This book is a discussion of problems relating to the four-year college of liberal arts and is written with the hope of contributing to a better public understanding and appreciation of the work of these institutions. The American college, especially the separately organized and privately supported college, is indigenous to the United States, and is one of the most important agencies our country has developed for preserving and making effective its basic social and political philosophy and the religious ideals that have led to the American way of life. The type of liberal education represented by these institutions can exist only in a democracy: freedom is their native air. Any interference or even supervision by government is incompatible with their spirit and if such controls should be exercised to any considerable extent that which is most distinctive and precious about them would perish.

What we have written may be regarded as an appeal to Americans to provide more adequate financial support for institutions of the college type in the various sections of the country to enable them to represent true college ideals and to offer full-rounded college opportunities to those sections and so to the nation as a whole.

The authors wish to thank the Carnegie Corporation of New York for having financed the writing of this book, and the Association of American Colleges for sponsoring its publication. The book is a collaboration based on ideas which have been forming in the authors' minds for fourteen years of close association—five years together at the same college, nine years as administrators of liberal arts colleges of the same type. Similarity of ideas early became apparent and has ripened with acquaintance, so that the book represents a true fusion of our points of view. We are jointly responsible for the opinions expressed.

DONALD J. COWLING
CARTER DAVIDSON

April 1, 1947

Contents

Colleges for Freedom

CHAPTER I

Freedom and the Individual

This book is an expression of faith—faith in the essentials of the Christian religion, in the basic principles of American democracy, and in the processes of liberal education. We do not identify these three fields one with another, but we recognize that their central interests overlap. The more we study the objectives of Christianity and democracy, the more clearly we see in them the goals of liberal education—especially as they relate to the individual and to his rights and duties.

Christianity is concerned with men and women as individuals, and the New Testament from beginning to end is an intensely individualistic book. Individual human consciousness is recognized as the scene of action of all spiritual forces and as the only temporal embodiment of ultimate values. Whatever helps men as individuals to achieve a fuller, richer life is good; whatever thwarts or degrades or embitters human life is wrong. We have here the ultimate criterion of morality, and the standard of judgment for all social conditions and customs, all movements and institutions including governments themselves. That civilization which provides best for the growth of the highest type of individual life—that system is the best and is the best expression of the teachings of Jesus.

"The Sabbath was made for man and not man for the Sabbath." This is a single illustration of Jesus' view—one applied to the religious institutions of his day. Take the principle that is involved in this illustration and apply it everywhere and you have the basic standard by which to judge all questions of right and wrong and to test all movements, all creeds and dogmas, all organizations—religious, commercial, industrial, and politi-

1

cal. There is within the confines of time nothing of ultimate worth except a person. All else is secondary. Churches, governments, business organizations, educational institutions, and all other human agencies have no other proper purpose than to serve to enlarge, to enrich, and to make more happy and satisfying the lives of men and women as individuals. There are about two billion such individuals living today on the face of the earth. The religion of Jesus is concerned with every one of them.

Organized Christianity has frequently adjusted itself to ideas and philosophies which are inconsistent with the teachings of Jesus. It is not enough that the welfare of men be professed as an objective, particularly when welfare is thought of in material terms—food, shelter, and clothing. "Your Father knoweth that ye have need of all these things." Material prosperity will come in abundance, as the history of America shows, when citizens organize themselves on the basis of sound principles, the basic one of which is intellectual and spiritual freedom. No form of social organization, whether in business, labor, or government, can be permanent which does not provide adequately for the freedom of the individuals whose lives are involved. Here we come upon the central problem of our time and of all times: How shall human beings organize themselves in communities, in states, and internationally to secure for themselves as individuals opportunities to realize life's highest values and purposes? America was founded in the belief that freedom represents the only road to the promised land.

American democracy begins with this assumption. It seeks to free the individual from tyranny; to protect him in his right to life, liberty, and the pursuit of happiness; to guarantee specific rights such as those appended to the Constitution of the United States in the first ten Amendments or the Bill of Rights; to implement the will of the majority without crushing the minority; to remove all artificial barriers to the full development of men. America has unbounded faith in the importance and worth of individual men and women. Our government is not a thing apart from the people. It is a government of individuals, by individuals under law, and for individuals, and we need to keep our feet firm on this bedrock of democracy. No organization, whether in business or in statecraft, can ever lift itself above the welfare and rights of individual men; nor can its existence be justified except as it serves to enlarge and enrich their individual lives. This is what institutions and organizations are for and this is the function of every form of government that deserves to be tolerated.

Liberal education carries this idea through to its conclusion. The paramount consideration in curriculum building, selection of faculty, and classroom instruction is the development of free men. Free men are those who are able to develop fully all the potentialities with which they have been endowed by Providence. Freedom has little meaning except in connection with the lives of men and women as individuals, and for them actually to be free is to maintain such relations with all the forces, material and spiritual, that operate within them and upon them as will result in the full functioning of each individual's powers and in the full realization of all his possibilities. The free life thus becomes the fulfilled life, and freedom the opened way to fulfillment.

Freedom is not opposed to discipline. On the contrary, it depends upon a willingness to obey. Obey what? The answer is simple in form: Obey the laws that are embodied within the nature of things. The railway locomotive which races along its track is obviously much freer than the locomotive which shakes off all controls and digs its wheels into the dirt. The tennis player who has laboriously practiced until he has perfected the needed co-ordinations has thereby made himself free to place his shots where he wishes and win the match. The writer who has conquered the conventions and laws of grammar is then free to delight the reader with a style of his own. Life is based upon laws which never came before a legislature but which no living being can escape, the laws of the universe. Philosophers and scientists have labored for centuries to discover these laws in order that we may conform our lives to them and utilize our knowledge of them to make life more comfortable and productive. Just as man is a complex but orderly microcosm of millions of perfectly integrated parts, so the physical universe is an even more exquisitely ordered pattern of infinite extent and complexity, a macrocosm of clearly defined unity with inexorable laws. The fitting of our delicate individualities into the intricate workings of this universe without tragic accident is a task requiring a high degree of skill and patience, obtainable only through discipline. "Our wills are ours to make them thine" is more than a pious Tennysonian platitude; it is common sense and necessity.

The laws that we must obey are embodied not only in the world of reality outside of ourselves, but also in the world that we find within our own conscious experience. The limits of our freedom and the possibilities of our individual development are set by the powers and potentialities that Providence has mixed into our individual natures. For some of us, there are visible physical handicaps; for others, invisible but equally real mental defects; for all of us, some quality emphasized at the expense of others. Our rights, our freedom of choice, our decisions, therefore, are circumscribed by the laws of our internal nature as well as by the edicts of the external universe.

In similar fashion our individual rights are circumscribed by the rights of others. Naturally there is an overlapping and conflict when two wills are exercised in the same direction; for purposes of peace and mutual helpfulness we have reduced individual autonomy from the status of absolute ruler to that of limited monarch, limited by the co-ordinate rights of others. Robinson Crusoe could stand on his desert isle and boast "I am the monarch of all I survey," but desert isles have gone out of fashion these days, and we are forced to consider the feelings of our apartment-house neighbors. At the lowest level of society, the rights of others are recognized only through fear of physical force. At a higher level, society has developed laws to control and decide conflicts. Many of our personal whims and desires are subordinated and brought in line with the rights of others by the devices of convention or etiquette, present in all levels from savagery to cultivated courtliness. At the highest stage, we place limitations upon our individual demands because we have achieved a sense of personal morality or duty; our conscience "feels better" if we give the other fellow a chance.

So far we have insisted that no individual is qualified to exercise his freedom intelligently unless he knows the laws of cause and effect that operate in nature and in man and can adapt himself to their workings, and unless he acknowledges and makes allowance for the rights and freedom of other individuals. A further step toward freedom is willingness and ability to accept responsibility for our actions; children may be willing but are unable, whereas most adults are able but reluctant. It is for this reason that the child must submit in many matters to the authority of his elders; until he has reached an age of accountability, he cannot accept full responsibility, and therefore cannot exercise complete freedom. Even the average college freshman is legally under age, financially unaccountable, politically unfranchised, and socially immature; therefore most colleges exercise controls "in loco parentis" during the freshman year, gradually releasing them as the student acquires maturity. However, college authorities, in managing such restrictions as may seem necessary in guiding youth toward maturity, should never lose sight of the goal of liberal education —the development of individuals who understand the implications of freedom and who are willing and able to be responsible for their own actions.

People who are unwilling to assume the responsibilities of freedom often find escape in an attitude of frustration and futility and feel that they can do nothing about it. "The fathers have eaten sour grapes, and the children's teeth are set on edge" was written twenty-five hundred years ago. The reply of the prophet was: "Every one shall die for his own iniquity: every man that eateth the sour grapes, his teeth shall be set on edge." There is abroad in the wind today an idea that society is "moving" in certain directions, as if some moon were pulling us like the tides. This force or social trend is, however, merely a figure of speech. The "public mind" is composed of the minds of individual people; no one is doing any behaving except individuals. Therefore, if we are not to be at the beck and call of every demagogue, citizens must be encouraged to assume responsibility for making decisions as individuals and must be educated to make right decisions and to choose with intelligence and purpose.

But even this is not enough. Democracy has within it an explosive idea, an idea which literally lifts us up—that every individual is a potential leader. In the nature of the case the vast majority in any population must be followers. Democracy depends upon the possibility of easy transfer from being a follower to being a leader and from leadership to a willing yielding of it to others. The distinctive features of democracy are closely related to the sources and quality of its leaders and to the intelligence and the spirit of those who follow. The most reassuring fact of American history is the leadership that our democracy has produced—Washington, Jefferson, and both Roosevelts from the aristocracy; Lincoln, Jackson, and Booker T. Washington from the "underprivileged." It is not necessary to think of leadership only in political terms, nor only at the highest levels. One can be a leader in the formulation of group opinion, in artistic appreciation, in church activities, in business, or in countless other fields. For the complete development and freedom of an individual, he must find some area in which he can lead, even though that leadership may be limited to a small group and to a minor area of action. Such an experience in the responsibilities of leadership will be of value not only in organizing and making effective his own powers, but also in helping him to understand the conditions under which a leader must work, thus enabling him to be a more intelligent follower, whose co-operation and loyalty will be something more than blind acceptance of domination or futile zeal for fantastic goals.

Christianity, democracy, and liberal education have as their common aim fullness of life for the individual. "I am come that they might have life, and that they might have it more abundantly," said Jesus, and he said this in the role of a teacher. "If ye continue in my word . . . ye shall know the truth, and the truth shall make you free." Nowhere else is man so encouraged to believe in his essential godlikeness as in the teachings of Jesus, and from no other source can he so fully gain the inspiration and daring necessary to conceive of himself as a free spirit. It is the primary responsibility of democratic government to organize and maintain conditions which are favorable for the exercise of individual freedom. It is the function of liberal education to help the individual gain for himself the experience of freedom, to understand its implications, and to assume its responsibilities.

CHAPTER II

Colleges and Religion

The founders of our American colleges were for the most part religious men. The charters of nearly all the early colleges stated explicitly that it was their aim to promote the Christian religion. In a book published in London in 1643, entitled *New England's First Fruits*, appears this statement: "After God had carried us safe to New England and we had builded our houses, reared convenient places for God's worship and settled the civil government, one of the next things we longed for and looked after was to advance learning and perpetuate it to posterity, dreading to leave an illiterate ministry to the Church when our present ministers shall lie in the dust." Such is the story of the beginning of the first college in America, Harvard, whose motto for three hundred years has been "For Christ and the Church." The same religious purpose is evident in the stories of the founding of Yale and Dartmouth by Congregational ministers, of William and Mary College in Virginia by Episcopalians, and of Princeton by Presbyterians; the Baptists founded Brown; King's College (now Columbia University), also Episcopalian, was established according to its first announcement "to teach and engage the children to know God in Jesus Christ," and Rutgers was undertaken by the Dutch Reformed Church primarily to train men for its ministry.

These eight colleges, all definitely religious in their origin, together with what is now the University of Pennsylvania, founded by Benjamin Franklin, in which the influence of the Quakers was not lacking, constitute the chief colleges that had been established and were at work before the Revolution. As the nation developed, this religious zeal continued; more than

8

a thousand colleges have been founded under church auspices and given support from church funds. Their purpose is well expressed in the inscription that may be found over the doorway of Columbia's Earl Hall. "That Religion and Education may go hand in hand and character grow with knowledge."

But clearly as the past has recognized the importance of education for religion, the religion of the future will depend even more upon the spiritual insight and understanding that education brings. For more than a century forces have been at work which have made the world a new place for us to live in. The beginnings of these forces are scattered and lie back, many of them, centuries ago; but they have been uniting and reinforcing one another and gathering momentum throughout the whole modern period, and their effects are now evident. These forces have led to discoveries and inventions; they have revolutionized the world of industry; they have changed our manner of living and have given us comforts and conveniences undreamed of a few generations ago. Science has shown us that the story of the earth on which we live is entirely different from what our fathers thought. Psychology and kindred studies have analyzed man's mental and social life and traced its genesis and development; the highest ranges of man's life—his sentiments and hopes and aspirations—are described and classified; our basic concepts and principles are proved to have had a history and are traced to their beginnings. The level of general education has been raised, and illiteracy is being banished from the masses. People have been encouraged to think for themselves and to rely on their own judgment.

The confidence that earlier generations had in the religious ideas which controlled their conduct was based largely upon their respect for authority. The spirit of their times was such that the Church could formulate its teachings in fixed dogmas which men obeyed, and the sure confidence and the unclouded faith they had in the teachings of their religion provided a firm foundation for their character and gave to their lives direction and strength. The spirit of our times is different. Acceptance of moral and religious teachings can no longer be brought about by appeals to dogmatic authority nor by telling people today what other people once believed. The method of direct and unquestioning faith—almost universally accepted before the development of modern science—is not the way that truth takes hold of many minds today. We have come to believe that the traditional attitude of accepting the results of the thinking of earlier generations as sacred and holding them free from critical examination and appraisal is a mistaken one. If there is any reason for regarding the results of the thinking of the past as sacred, there is even greater reason for regarding our own right to think as still more sacred. We are in a better position today to have sound opinions about matters of health and of education and about questions relating to our industrial, social, economic, and political welfare than any previous generation has ever been in. No exception can be made in the case of religion. In every field of human interest we have a wider range of understanding and a truer perspective than the people of any earlier age have ever had. We no longer use the thinking of the past as a standard to judge the thinking of today; we use the thinking of today as the standard by means of which to test and appraise the thinking of the past. Our point of view cannot be reconciled with any attempt to regard the results of past thinking as sacred in themselves, nor with any appeal to people's sentiments and loyalties to hold on to accepted ideas for their own sake. We believe that there is no good reason why we should accept any idea in any field whatsoever except as we are persuaded that it is true, that it is the best idea to hold, that action based upon it will meet our needs today and add to our happiness.

We need not fear the spirit or methods of our times. When accepted and followed, they constitute a surer approach to truth than the intellectual controls of earlier ages. The only ground for fear is that when authority is relaxed no adequate education—the only alternative—will take its place. As an illustration of this reason for concern, let us take the attitude of many people toward the Bible. We need not go back very far to the time when men believed that the Bible came direct from God in the precise form in which it now stands, that its writers simply wrote down what was dictated by its divine author, and that not only the principles and ideas but the very words and phrases came direct from God himself. In simple and unquestioning faith our fathers accepted this doctrine of the verbal and literal inspiration of the Scriptures and, believing in their inerrancy in all matters of history and science as well as religion, they revered the Book and obeyed its precepts. But the time came when science called in question many things which had passed as true; and when the history of the Bible was studied by methods used in other fields, it was found to be in many respects quite different from what had been supposed.

We know now that the Bible is not a source of knowledge about scientific matters, and that the scientific conceptions in which the Biblical writers clothed their thoughts were held in common with other men of their time and were those of the age in which they lived. Joshua, for example, believed that the sun moved around the earth, and the writer of Genesis believed that the world was created in six days marked by morning and evening. Modern science has long since outgrown these conceptions, and the achievements of recent scientists have completely antiquated many of the scientific notions of even a few years ago. These negative results of modern scholarship have been in reality a great positive boon, for by taking away they have greatly added. The Bible in some respects is not what it was thought to be, but it is now a great deal more; namely, what it actually is. By lifting the accumulations of tradition, modern study has disclosed the altogether unique religious value of the Bible, which is making a fresh appeal today and is challenging acceptance as the surest guide to a freer and fuller life for individuals and to lasting peace. The Bible now means most to those who intelligently understand it.

What is true of many people's attitude toward the Bible is equally true of their attitude toward the other great teachings of the Church, which throughout the centuries have been regarded as essential for man's welfare and happiness. Multitudes of people have given up their simple and direct faith in religious teachings but have not been trained to understand the principles and processes involved in the attainment of worthy ideals of character and goodness. The hope for the future lies in education—in the schools, in homes, and in more effective programs of education in the churches—and for the realization of this hope the influence and leadership of the colleges are more needed than ever.

What is there for colleges to teach about religion? Their programs should be based on the teachings of Jesus, which have to do chiefly with interpretations in three main areas of belief: how—in what terms—are we to conceive of the vast stretches of reality that we call the universe, what is the nature of man, and what basis is there for appraising what man regards as right or wrong?

The universe in which we live is a vast and complicated whole. There is nothing in it that exists separate and apart, or by or for itself alone. Every particle of reality bears some relation to every other, and is dependent upon all others to a greater or less extent. Even the word "universe" implies the essential unity of all reality; it is a unified, living organism. However, we cannot comprehend it as a whole. We go about our study of it piecemeal. We study the universe from a certain angle and set our findings in order and call them "astronomy"; we shift our point of view and systematize the results of our study and call them "physics"; and so through all the circle of the sciences. It has happened in a few cases that a wonderfully gifted man in the short period of his own lifetime has been able to discover nearly all we know about the universe in a limited area. Euclid practically accomplished this in plane geometry, and Aristotle in deductive logic. In most cases it has taken a great many men, working through long periods of time, to tell us what we know about the universe in particular fields. However, in all science, whether developed by the marvelous insight of some great genius or by the patient and prolonged plodding of less gifted men, there is implied a universe which behaves rationally, which has its laws and principles, and which makes demands that are not to be avoided. Our freedom in these areas consists in finding out what these laws are and in fashioning our behavior in accordance with them.

The province of science is description, not explanation; it deals with sequences, not causes. When science has told its story there remain at least two questions unanswered for which no answer can be found by its methods: the question of the first origin of things and the question of the inner essence and nature of force. Granted a beginning and granted a power at work, science does tell in marvelous fashion of the unfolding of that power and of the wonderful forms in which it manifests itself in the physical world; but it cannot go beyond this. Any satisfactory answer to the question of first origins or to the question of the ultimate nature of force carries us far beyond the realm of science.

Religion's most important contribution to human thought is monotheism. The words "universe" and "monotheism" belong together; they are coextensive, and the meaning of the second is embodied in the first. Monotheism assumes that the universe is best conceived of in personal terms; that back of the phenomena of nature which we see around us is conscious intelligence; that underneath and within the facts of the physical world is the everlasting Spirit, and that at the heart of reality is the eternal self. God is universal and within his will are the principles and values that make of the physical universe a moral order in which all mankind is involved and through which all individuals attain their destiny.

This is the view of Jesus. He never argued about the existence of God. He was aware of him as a great present reality in his own experience. He not only takes it for granted that the universe at heart is a person, but conceives of him in terms of all that is highest and best in human life: God is a Father whose nature is love, and kindness and mercy, patience and long-suffering are his essential attributes. The whole sum total of reality is permeated, through and through, with the spirit and purposes of this God of love.

This is the first and most important of the teachings of Jesus. What he said about men and women and children as individuals is the other side of what he said about God. God is the Father of all mankind and therefore all men are his children. No human being is outside the Father's love and care. Every individual shares in the conscious life of God and is of infinite concern to the Father in heaven. In all the relations that men establish with each other this central conviction must be our guide. No relationship is right which is inconsistent with it, and in its fulfillment all the ends of individual life and human society will be realized.

Jesus lived at a time when mechanical religious rites were allowed as substitutes for the performance of moral obligations. "Woe unto you, Pharisees! for ye tithe mint and rue and all manner of herbs, and pass over justice and the love of God." No amount of religious professionalism will take the place of the things of the spirit, and there is no virtue whatever in external performance for its own sake. It is not in outward conformity but in inward obedience that the demands of the good life are met; and the quality of love is the essence of all moral worth.

These are the essential teachings of Jesus. The greatest question before the world today is "Is Jesus to be trusted?" Do we find in his teachings and in his spirit foundations upon which we can build, or was he mistaken? The most profound and far-reaching claim Jesus ever made concerning himself was that he spoke for God. "My teaching is not mine, but his that sent me." "I and my Father are one; He that seeth me, seeth the Father." Jesus not only understands the attributes and the will of God; he embodies them; he makes them live in his own life and in his teachings. He is literally a revelation of God.

Jesus never claimed to be a dictator of moral values; but he did claim to be sensitive and responsive to the moral and spiritual laws of the universe, and that these essential principles are interpreted in a reliable and dependable way in his teachings and in the spirit of his life: "If any man thirst, let him come unto me and drink"; "I am the bread of life"; "I am the light of the world." The validity of Jesus' claims does not rest on ecclesiastical authority or pronouncements but on the nature of the results of action based on an acceptance of his teachings: "If any man will do his will, he shall know of the teaching, whether it be of God, or whether I speak of myself." This is the core of the Christian doctrine of the deity of Jesus—that his teachings are more than his personal opinions or the opinions approved by the authorities of his day—they belong to the inner nature of things and are wrought into the structure of ultimate reality.

All through the teachings of Jesus is the assumption that at the heart of reality there is intelligence and character, purpose and good will; and that men and women, as individuals, achieve their possibilities and their destiny only when by their "soul's sincere desire"—which is the essence of prayer—and by the resulting choices they seek to bring their lives into relations of correspondence with these inner attributes of reality—that is, with God, and thus to do his will. St. Augustine, in the first chapter of the Confessions, says: "Thou hast made us for thyself, and our hearts are restless 'til they find rest in Thee." Embodied in man are godlike qualities: love and unceasing outreaching for truth, beauty, and goodness. Until a person finds these realized in what he does and in his relations with other men he is dissatisfied, his heart is restless, and he seeks after a better way of life and a better world.

What is true of the lives of men and women as individuals is true also of the groups they form, and of the institutions they devise to further the interests of their common life. The lasting satisfactions of life, both for individuals and for groups, including nations, can be attained only when their activities are carried on in accordance with the inner nature of reality, in obedience to the laws and principles that constitute the essence of existence—that is, in obedience to the will of God. David Lloyd George, after World War I, while he was still prime minister of Great Britain, issued a proclamation from which the following sentences are taken: "It has become clear today . . . that neither education, science, diplomacy, nor commercial prosperity, when allied with a belief in material force as the ultimate power, are real foundations for the ordered development of the world's life. These things are in themselves simply the tools of the spirit that handles them. . . . The spirit of goodwill among men rests on spiritual forces; the hope of a 'brotherhood of humanity' reposes on the deeper spiritual fact of the 'Fatherhood of God.' In the recognition of the fact of that Fatherhood and of the Divine purpose for the world which are central to the message of Christianity, we shall discover the ultimate foundation for the reconstruction of an ordered and harmonious life for all men. . . . We believe that in the acceptance of those spiritual principles lies the sure basis of world peace."

Mankind has been slow in believing this or in trusting any such belief as a basis for action. The relations between nations have been conducted almost universally upon the basis of selfishness and force. These have been justified in the name of patriotism, which in international relations has seldom represented anything more admirable than narrow and bigoted nationalism. International policies based on selfishness and force are doomed and always have been doomed. There has never from the beginning been any real possibility of developing a happy and satisfying life among men on the basis of these essentially wrong ideas. It is because men, clothed with the authority of nationalism, have been unwilling to recognize this simple truth that they have continuously, generation after generation, involved millions of their fellow countrymen in agony and in a fruitless quest for security and a happy life. The problems that so sorely trouble the world today, problems of management and labor, problems of race, of social levels and special privileges, of nationalism and international relations, all these and other problems will be solved eventually in accordance with the essential teachings of Jesus, for the simple reason that the universe is built that way. "God is not mocked," and in the long run his will prevails. No civilization can stand permanently until it is based on spiritual principles and brought into harmony with the will of God.

American colleges almost without exception were founded to train leaders in the Christian way of life and to strengthen the influence of spiritual forces in our country. They have been responsible to a large extent for the ideals America has cherished and are more needed than ever to maintain and to extend the faith of our people in these ideals as the only sure guide for organizing the affairs of men.

CHAPTER III

Colleges and American Democracy

American democracy is more than a system of political citizenship. It is a way of life. It is essentially a moral order based on freedom of decision, on voluntary action under moral responsibility. It is a democratic society of individuals equal before the law, living under a republican form of government, with officials elected as representatives, and with checks and balances between executive, judiciary and legislature, between the Senate and the House, between the federal government and the states, between the states themselves, between the state and the counties and townships, with authority resting finally on no one but the people. It is not a democratic social scheme under communism or monarchy or fascism or bureaucracy, but under a carefully planned republic.

The American way of life implies freedom to move about, to travel without the typical European registration regulations or confinement to ghettos. It implies freedom to choose one's own companions regardless of their social status or the caste or class to which they or we may have been born: this includes marriage, for Americans are accustomed to choose their own wives and husbands and not leave such matters to government officials or parents. It includes the right "to live alone and like it," not to be forced into mass action; to spend one's income as one desires, and not as the government commands; to live according to one's own standards of comfort and convenience, instead of the regulations of bureaucracy; and to seek out forms of recreation and enjoyment suited to one's taste, not such as are prescribed by the official committee. It means the right to think for one's self, to express freely one's own convictions, and to follow such patterns of religious practice as one may choose.

American freedom implies more than political freedom or social rights; it means economic freedom also. From the earliest days of the Republic, Americans have felt free to work if and when they pleased; to accept employment from another or to work for oneself or to establish a business and employ others; to change occupation if it seemed desirable to do so. Although during wartime it may have been expedient to "freeze" men in their jobs, such cannot be a peacetime American practice. For many years past, three great forces have been operating to destroy economic freedom in America and to substitute control by force:

The first of these, in point of time, is the corporation. America could not have attained its present position of industrial supremacy without the corporation or some similar institution which permits the accumulation of capital from thousands of individuals while concentrating the managerial function in the hands of a few. This arrangement appears to be essential for efficient administration. However, it affords opportunity for undue selfishness on the part of those managements which ignore the sound principle that power carries with it social responsibilities. A recent president of the United States Chamber of Commerce says: "The old capitalism was monopolistic; it stifled competition and thereby throttled opportunity for the little fellow." Probably the period that witnessed the most flagrant disregard of individual rights by corporate managements was the Trust Era of the latter decades of the nineteenth century and the early years of the twentieth. Mammoth corporations were formed for the purpose of securing monopoly control of various products in order to acquire monopoly profits. As a reaction, first some of the states, and then the federal government, passed legislation which declared these giants to be in restraint of trade and ordered them, in the interest of the public, to be broken up.

This proved to be a lengthy process. The states generally have tended to abandon their responsibilities in this field and to leave the controls to the federal government, which, before it became at all effective, had to develop better enforcement agencies, a more consistent attitude on the part of the courts, and numerous amendments to earlier laws. Governmental philosophy and public attitude have become more sensitive in the past generation or two to the economic rights of individual citizens. The Clayton Act, Fair Practices Act, and the Robinson-Patman Act are examples of legislative attempts to protect the individual.

Many corporations employ legal staffs to tell them just where the line is between what is legal and what is illegal and their policy seems to be to go just as far as the law allows. In some cases the primary duty of these legal staffs is to keep their companies technically within the law without regard to its intent. Attempts are made to reinterpret, or even sidestep, legislative enactments, so that in some areas corporations still have monopolistic control and it is practically impossible for anyone to set up a new business. In other fields the market has been divided among a few mammoth corporations, via the cartel, so that any smaller enterprise is squeezed out.

Threats to personal rights come from small as well as large business interests. The large American corporation is easy to find, its accounts are well kept and available to the scrutiny of public officials. On the other hand, small companies may escape public attention and legal action against them is less spectacular and newsworthy. A combination of small companies operating within a state may show no interstate aspects which permit the intervention of federal authorities.

How promptly such conditions result in corrective governmental action depends upon the efficiency of the agencies and the political policy of the party in power. Unfortunately, governmental policy has not always been consistent. It is essential that individual citizens, in jealously guarding their liberties, constantly prod their public servants to vigilance and action. However, no real solution to such problems will ever be found until corporation executives, directors, and stockholders are educated to a realization of their responsibility toward American freedom for all persons. They must learn to work under the motivation of ideals, just as all individuals must; otherwise our private business economy may face destruction.

Second in order, labor organizations have tried to dominate and control. The issues of the closed shop, the checkoff system, and the limit on apprentices are too vivid in the public mind to require amplification. It is understandable how union methods were forced upon them by employers' tactics, and every American is sympathetic with the laborer's desire for a living wage. But, now that the unions include almost all laborers in the major industries, the days of the strong-arm promoters would seem to be passing. Labor now needs a new type of leader, liberally educated and professionally trained. The problems involved in our industrial and commercial life are as complicated and technical when viewed from the standpoint of labor as from that of management, and require for their proper settlement labor leaders who are as able and well trained as are business executives. For our economic well-being it is as necessary for the president of the union to be educated to his opportunities and responsibilities as it is for the president of the corporation. The colleges must provide suitable educational opportunities for training such leaders of labor.

The federal government, the third party now threatening American economic freedom, has expanded tremendously in power during the past decade. Its appetite has now grown to terrific proportions. The industrialists and financiers and corporations had by far the best of the arrangements during the nineteenth century, but today labor has attained power more devastating in some respects than that ever possessed by capital. As long as the federal government remains the arbiter of disputes between the other two, there is some chance for justice, but the present tendency is for government itself to go into business as a competitor of existing corporations and to assume authority for the settlement of disputes which should be left to free negotiation between the parties concerned under suitable government regulations. Caught in the push among these three, the individual is likely to lose his freedom to work and his other rights. When three parties are fighting, there are likely to be coalitions of two against one. If government lines up with labor, the country moves toward a "dictatorship of the proletariat," or state socialism, and the individual disappears; if government combines with capital, fascism emerges and the individual again is crushed. Our federal government was not designed to compete with business or to organize labor, but to preserve the freedom of the individual.

It is one of the main purposes of liberal education in America to develop men and women who understand what American democracy means—the assumptions on which it is based, its implications and responsibilities, and the necessary but limited place that government holds in such a way of life. Do our colleges today actually develop such leaders? Does the education which students in our colleges receive increase their devotion to American ideals and their faith in freedom as the way of gaining what men should have, or do they find all the other isms presented in such an attractive manner, and our own way so maligned, that their loyalties are shaken? Do the freedoms permitted to college students leave them confused and undisciplined, or do our young men and women come out of college with clearer minds and deeper faith because they have been unhampered by totalitarian restrictions?

Every time this subject is mentioned some college and university faculty members begin to feel uneasy. They insist that the democratic spirit is a by-product, not the result of direct indoctrination. As a matter of fact, they say, indoctrination is the denial of freedom, and therefore impossible in a true democracy. College teachers can point with pride to the record of service by college graduates and students during World War II, and say this is their vindication—what better evidence can a man give of his faith in democracy than by his willing devotion to its defense? Americans, as a nation, have shown themselves quite as patriotic as any other warring people. But, says the New York *Times,* our high school and college graduates are woefully ignorant of the facts of American history and the principles embodied in our Constitution; therefore, education has failed the nation. Many high schools do not require courses in American history for a diploma, and as a result colleges cannot insist upon such courses for admission, though they are highly recommended. College curricula do not usually contain required courses in American history; but the same thing could be said of mathematics or physics or almost any other particular course. It is safe to say, however, that the college graduate who has never come in contact with American history in either high school or college is the rare exception rather than the rule.

If this is so, remarks the *Times,* how is it possible for the student to be so ignorant that he credits Jefferson with the founding of the *Saturday Evening Post* and calls Theodore Roosevelt the head of the NRA? Surely no one would believe that he was actually taught such things in history class! Boners are uttered and written every day in every subject—none more frequently than in mathematics and English, which are taught from the first grade up. A student will continue to derive jumbled ideas about American history and government even if required courses in these subjects should be legislated into every year of the curriculum. Ideas will be thrown at him from the newspapers, radio, pulpit, movies, and conversations on the street, and he may occasionally read a historical romance or even a biography. Is there any wonder that he becomes confused, and insists that Alexander Hamilton and Benjamin Disraeli looked alike because George Arliss played both roles?

It is a recognized principle of psychology that our convictions and impressions vary in power according to their original vividness or intensity, their recency, and the frequency with which they are experienced or recollected. Our colleges, therefore, should seek to make their presentation of the essential ideas of American democracy an interesting and vivid experience for their students and should repeat and recall them frequently, weaving them into all the personal loyalties that the student acquires. This cannot be done through a single course. It has been suggested that each college appoint a professor of American Studies qualified to interpret the philosophical and religious assumptions on which our government is based, to trace the workings of these convictions in the development of our political, economic, and cultural methods and institutions, and to help the student understand what our basic ideas mean in terms of the problems that face us today. Such a member of the faculty would secure the co-operation of his colleagues in many fields and would be chiefly responsible for a program of studies in which many departments would participate.

The content of such instruction would grow from the body of materials that make America a nation. First of all, Americans are bound together by a common past, stretching back through more than three centuries on this continent, and stemming from an Anglo-Saxon tradition of a thousand years more. We have shared a common struggle and common dangers to become a nation, and to keep that nation united. Certain nuclear individuals like Washington and Lincoln we have grown to love; we join hands with them and say "it happened to us" or "these things we have done together." Therefore the first emphasis would be upon the great personalities, political, military, scientific, literary, who have given new meaning and luster to the name "American" and who bind us to themselves in a lasting fellowship. Also the great events, such as historic battles, constitutional conventions, crucial elections, judicial decisions, can be described so vividly that they will remain forever engraved on the student's memory.

Our nation is held together by all this, and by constant reminders of the ties that bind. Washington and Lincoln's birthdays, Memorial Day, the Fourth of July, Labor Day, and Thanksgiving are quite as important to the preservation of our national consciousness as are Christmas and Easter to the life of the Christian Church. When these occasions appear on the calendar, the faculty and students should not consider them merely holidays with freedom from classes, but should celebrate them as opportunities to renew our national loyalties.

How does American democracy function? It is not chaotic license and planlessness, nor merely a device for voting and representation; rather it is a spirit of social behavior, refusing to give arbitrary power to any individual or group, but relying on free discussion and consensus of judgment. We began as a "cracker-barrel" democracy, and the great addresses from Samuel Adams on down through the Constitutional Convention, Webster and Clay and Calhoun, to the Lincoln-Douglas debates should be studied intensively, for they set the pattern of public discussion, carried on in the "lyceums," intercollegiate and interscholastic debates, open forums, radio town meetings, and letters to the press of later days. There is particular need of this discussion today, because our congressmen have shifted from the old Edmund Burke theory of a "representative expressing his own opinion" to the McKinley doctrine of "keeping his ear to the ground of public desires."

What elements of the law should a citizen know in order to protect himself and his neighbor? How do our American courts operate? A visit to the county courthouse during an interesting trial case would not be amiss. What part can the average intelligent citizen play in the politics of his community, state, and nation? What is peculiarly American about our public school system, the relation of church and state, and other institutions public and private? How has the American economic system come into existence, and what problems are before it for solution?

We must follow our students into their home communities, to see how they approach their duties as citizens. While they are in college, the summer vacations could provide a practical introduction to community service for many a future voter. It would undoubtedly be very revealing to the average college to make a survey of the alumni, asking such questions as: In what percentage of the elections held since you reached voting age have you actually voted? Are you a party member? Do you vote regularly in the primaries? Do you participate in the party councils? Have you ever run for office? What offices have you held? In these activities have you been influenced by what you learned in college? In what way? Perhaps on the basis of the replies to such a questionnaire, a valuable course of study could be built.

The America in which our graduates will live, however, will be held together by its hopes for the future quite as much as by its memories of the past. Every great nation must have long-term and long-distance goals. We used to speak glibly of our "manifest destiny." Although it may no longer be quite so manifest, our destiny as a nation is certainly a matter for deep concern. A professor of American Studies might well show how through all the changing scenes and problems of our national life, our goals have remained the same; from the past he might venture to project our goals into the future; what kind of America should our college graduates strive to build?

Again, what is there about Americans that sets them apart from other people? What is the essence of the American psy-

chology? What national types have we developed—the fron-
tiersman, the industrial leader, the professional reformer, and
others? It would be valuable to study what contributions each
immigrant group has made to the modern America.

Also, what kind of world should America try to help create?
No liberal education could sincerely inculcate chauvinism or
selfish isolationism, a feeling that we are the chosen people. In
the creation and strengthening of loyalties, the teacher must
not stop at the national border. The fact that we are devoted to
our own family does not prevent our seeking also the welfare
of our neighbors. Our interest in the home town does not conflict with our devotion to the home state. Since the Civil War
settled the issue, allegiance to Illinois or Virginia does not interfere with national patriotism. In like manner, to carry the
argument to its logical conclusion, fealty to the United States
of America should merely serve to intensify our desire for a
world of peace and harmony and co-operative brotherhood.
Liberal education supports those who seek to liberate mankind
from narrow and selfish provincialism and helps us to see the
welfare of men everywhere as a common cause.

Surely a professor of American Studies would never lack
materials for his teaching; his main task would be selection.
Would his work conflict with that of the teachers of American
history, government, economics, and literature? There should
be no conflict, only supplementation and a different emphasis.
Our colleges must face this task of education in American democracy with conviction and resolution. We have spent great
efforts on the Americanization of immigrants, but have neglected to make the native citizen acquainted with his birthright.
The liberal arts college believes in the supreme importance of
the individual in a democratic society; with its chief purpose
centering in the development of the individual, it is perhaps
the best of all our educational agencies for implementing this
belief in American democracy. There are rumors abroad that

our American loyalties are moving away from individualism toward stateism and bureaucracy. If this be true, then the task of the college is clear—to exert every effort toward returning America to faith in individual freedom and in democratic constitutional government.

CHAPTER IV

How the Individual Achieves Maturity

Most parents want their children to "grow up" into well-balanced adults. If this process is going to take place automatically, they have nothing to worry about. If well-rounded mature individuals arrive at that state merely by the passage of time, education has no important function. But even in savage society it was necessary for the young to be taught the approved methods of self-preservation. As civilization advances it becomes more complex and complicated, a condition which requires a longer period of adaptation. We must, therefore, ask ourselves how the individual achieves maturity and what education contributes to the process.

Some maturity is achieved merely with the passage of time. The adult should know more than the child, or what is maturity for? We all sympathize with Bronson Alcott, our early American "progressive" educator, who sat with his seven-year-old pupils in the Hall of Philosophy at Concord and plied them with questions about their innate knowledge of heaven, but we cannot believe the advancement of learning was great in that process. Wordsworth may have felt "intimations of immortality from recollections of early childhood" and collected the sayings of infants in the hope that some secret might be discovered before the "shades of the prison house begin to close upon the growing boy," but the poet was no pragmatist. Education can have little meaning unless it is based upon the supposition that the adult can and should know more than the child. But this greater knowledge will not be achieved merely by a laissez-faire program of allowing little Mary to unfold her petals effortlessly to the sun. It must be carefully planned and cultivated every step of the way.

Education must begin with the body. The tool of health and physical vigor is quite as important as language or manual skill, and just as difficult to maintain. As one looks around, he is shocked by the poor physiques, the frequent illnesses, and the early loss of vitality in middle age. The Second World War has again made clear the fact that many Americans do not look after themselves properly, so that a high percentage are not fit even to carry a gun. Colleges with varying degrees of adequacy have provided health programs for their students for several generations past. Statistics show that the health of college-trained people is distinctly better than that of the population as a whole. It could perhaps be proved that four years of properly utilized health facilities in a good college will add four years to the life expectancy of the student if the habits there learned are continued afterward; thus college years are not taken out of life, but are added to it.

Good health is rooted in a reasonable inheritance of sound body and mind. Retaining and improving health calls for an individualized program of positive action. Mind and body must be disciplined, exercised, and protected in such ways as will allow each to function fully with the minimum of wear and tear. Since such vital preparation for living should not be left to chance, or perhaps bitter experience, a college should recognize the instructional aspects of health as one of its prime obligations; it should strive to stimulate a wholesome attitude toward health preservation during college years in the hope that this outlook will be maintained and further developed later. A modern educational program must include such instruction if it is to meet the needs of tomorrow's citizens and equip them for the problems, personal and community, they will be called upon to face.

Before prospective students leave their homes, the well-organized college health service has already set in motion its plan of close co-operation with family physicians by establishing contacts with the doctor, whose years of ministering to the student and the student's family have placed him in a peculiarly advantageous and informed position. His interest and aid have been invited in seeing to it that young people who plan to come to college are in good physical condition before they are deprived temporarily of close association with their families and their accustomed physician. Having arrived at college, each new student receives the first of his thorough annual physical examinations, careful records being kept on file for future reference. The student is informed of the results of the examination in a constructive personal conference that represents his first intimate contact with the physician who will be his close medical adviser throughout his college course. Where the examination reveals findings that obviously should be communicated to the parents or family physician, this procedure is promptly carried out.

Based on the findings at entrance and later examinations, individualized recommendations are made concerning athletics, programs of exercise, and other matters pertaining to health. A student in good physical condition is permitted to participate in any activity he prefers. Those with minor defects will be kept out of heavy contact sports, and those needing corrective exercise and attention will be carefully advised in the selection of their work and supervised in the carrying out of remedial programs.

Intramural activities, which should include the entire student body, provide an outlet for voluntary interest; such a program is the natural outgrowth of physical education instruction because once students have mastered the skills of their chosen sports they naturally desire opportunities for actual experience in them. Thus pleasurable recreation, the development of ability to win or lose gracefully, the benefits that come with hard, clean competition are all placed within reach of many students who might find it quite impossible to qualify for intercollegiate athletics.

Contests in a wide variety of sports between institutions of the same type are of great interest to those who take part in them and add much to the pleasure of the whole student body. Colleges are in a much better position to provide some form of intercollegiate competition for most of their students than are institutions with larger enrollments. Instead of concentrating on one sport a season, with football, basketball, and track drawing off most of the players of ability, a college should provide a half dozen intercollegiate sports each season: soccer, rifle, cross-country, golf, tennis, and football in the fall; hockey, indoor track, swimming, badminton, squash rackets, boxing, wrestling, and basketball in the winter; baseball, track, tennis, golf, lacrosse, and crew in the spring.

Suitable insignia should be awarded for satisfactory service on any team. Instead of judging the success or failure of a season upon the basis of the number of victories and losses, let the mark of success be the number of individuals competing, the number of contests held, the number of letters awarded. Such games in the smaller colleges are not likely to be events of great public interest, nor should athletic victories be regarded as important in the public relations programs of these institutions; they should be maintained primarily for the health and physical welfare of the individuals who participate in them, and no other advantage should ever be sought at the expense of this objective.

Colleges should not be judged by the winning records of their teams, nor the size of the gymnasium and playing fields; but there is no injustice in demanding a diversified, well-established, competently staffed, and individualized program of physical education as a test of a good college. The purpose of such a program is to give opportunities for exercise adequate for the development of a healthy individual and to provide instruction and direction in skills or activities which will prove of real value after graduation. The aim is to make attractive recreation habits that will not be forgotten as soon as the spur of requirement is no longer felt. It is recognized that there exists a close relationship between experience and skill in games or other forms of exercise and the enjoyment of them by the participant. Students are therefore encouraged to attain more than the skill of a novice in several activities and to gain sufficient liking for at least one to continue participation in it during later life.

A knowledge of games and skill in their execution should enable college-trained people, whatever their vocation may be, to balance against the stresses and strains of mature responsibility the restorative and tonic release offered by regular recreation. Regular participation in some form of physical expression not only increases the individual's effectiveness in whatever he undertakes, but also his feeling of confidence and well-being, and adds variety and enjoyment to living. The character effects of such participation should also be kept in mind. It is difficult to see how a student can take part in a properly directed program of physical exercise and competitive sports without developing qualities of character greatly needed in adult life—initiative and resourcefulness functioning under rules and later under law, self-discipline resulting in self-control in particular situations, patience and endurance necessary to complete an undertaking, and willingness to work with others in the realization of common ends.

A fully developed college health service should include a dental section. At least once each year a college should require each student to have, as a companion piece of investigation to his annual medical examination, a thorough dental survey, including a complete set of dental radiographs. If any defects are found, as they commonly are, they should be carefully explained to the student, along with the importance of having them properly looked after at once. The activities of a college in this field may well be confined to diagnostic work, the student being requested to have the necessary work attended to by a dentist of his own choice. By following this program an early and essentially complete diagnosis is assured, corrective procedures are possible before it is too late, and another vital point in the protection of student health has been covered. These steps should be supplemented and reinforced by individual discussions of dental prophylaxis with small groups. The practicing dentists in the community will probably be glad to assist in the program by part-time service.

In addition to the immediate and personal services afforded students by the college health service and the instruction and recreation offered by the physical education program, a well-developed college health program should include two further types of health training. For the prospective professional workers who will later complete their courses in schools of medicine, dentistry, nursing, or the allied sciences, the necessary preprofessional courses should be available. A very different and not nearly so specialized type of training is needed, however, by those whose responsibility for health will be in connection with family and community life, welfare work, schools, or in the business world. With approaching responsibility for family health just ahead, students realize the need for health conservation and seek the information and insight that will enable them to select their future medical advisers wisely and co-operate with them intelligently. The training offered is founded upon the fundamental sciences of anatomy, physiology, physiological chemistry, bacteriology, and pathology. Important basic contributions from these subjects are studied, new discoveries discussed, and salient truths indicated as logical guides to the surest methods of conserving health.

Supervisory oversight of institutional factors bearing on

health, such as food and water supplies, heat, moisture, ventilation and cleanliness of buildings, should be maintained. Through office conferences, by means of frequent talks before interested groups, and by using the medium of the college student paper, a positive health program may be kept constantly before both students and faculty. To be effective, health habits must become an accepted and almost unconscious part of the daily routine.

A college cannot escape its responsibility for the physical welfare and development of its students; but this is not its chief purpose. "Mens sana in corpore sano" is still pertinent and colleges are concerned with both body and mind, but they are organized primarily for the training of the mind. When we talk of expanding and strengthening the mind we must be careful of our language. There is still a great deal of uncertainty about the nature of mental processes, the transfer of training, and the levels of learning. What are the intellectual powers that can be improved? Obviously the moron cannot achieve the higher mental processes; but what can we expect of the average student? Beavers and rattlesnakes can adapt themselves beautifully to their environment; savage man conforms religiously to the mores of the tribe; robots and machinery surpass man in the performance of technical tasks. It is man's mental powers that make possible his superiority. What are they? How can they be improved? The following list, arranged approximately in ascending order of difficulty, indicates the more essential capacities of the human mind:

(1) The ability to concentrate attention upon the matter under consideration, recognizing the problem to be solved. Students frequently complain that their attention wanders from the page and they wake up with the realization that no impression has been made upon the mind. Distractions of noise and movement often prevent complete concentration, though we have all heard stories of people who are able to concentrate

their attention under the most unfavorable circumstances. During the war the air forces developed methods of teaching aircraft identification which developed the power of concentrated attention remarkably; in the pilot's seat, one slight lapse might spell disaster. The science laboratory has proved an excellent place for teaching concentration. It might be plausibly argued that certain subjects which are definitely boring or exceptionally difficult for the student have a high educational value because they make it necessary for him to concentrate his attention to an unusual degree if he is to get anything out of them. Concentration of attention is probably the most elementary in the scale of higher mental processes, but without this accomplishment the student will find the others almost impossible of attainment.

(2) Accuracy in observation—the ability to see similarities and differences. The average witness in an accident case cannot be sure that the automobile was green or brown, turned right or left, was a Buick or a Chrysler. A popular after-dinner game is to show a picture for two or three minutes to your guests, then hide the picture and ask them twenty questions about the features in it. "Funny, but I didn't notice that," will be the characteristic reaction. Mathematics, accounting, statistics, comparative anatomy, and foreign language study can do much to improve the student's accuracy; a slight difference in spelling may make a vast difference in meaning, one almost imperceptible physical characteristic may mark a different species.

(3) A retentive memory—the power of "recovery," or selective recall. The old-fashioned education placed perhaps undue emphasis upon this mental accomplishment, but our modern way errs just as far in the opposite direction. Perhaps the appreciation of literature was in an earlier day spoiled by the memorizing of hundreds of lines of verse, but the situation today can hardly be regarded as better when a student shows no spark of recognition of a quotation from the Bible, Shake-

speare, or the Declaration of Independence. To be a good mathematician, it is not necessary to memorize the logarithmic tables, but it helps considerably to remember a few formulas. Dates, the names of kings, and map study may be a bore to the history student, but it is hard to grant that intelligence exists in a person who places Paris in the Scandinavian peninsula or makes contemporaries of Queen Elizabeth and Napoleon. Thomas Babington Macaulay won many a debate in Parliament by his remarkable ability to quote the statutes verbatim though impromptu. More than one politician has used the power to remember names and faces to place him in public office. Memory cannot be "strengthened" by meaningless exercises, but many useful facts can be stored away for future reference by conscious use of the memory Even though we may never be invited to appear with "Information Please" or questioned by Doctor I.Q., it still remains true that minds which are richly stored with facts represent soil from which new ideas are more likely to spring than from barren ground.

(4) Sensitivity to association. A student who is able to concentrate, observe, and memorize may be severely handicapped by insensitivity. Tests indicate that this is a quality which can be improved by training. In the arts it is what Shakespeare and his contemporaries called "fancy." It has resulted in figures of speech such as the metaphor and the simile, which are merely perceptions of association. In science it may take the form of perceiving new combinations and relationships which lead to the invention of new machines, processes, and products; it is the power possessed in highly developed form by Edison, Steinmetz, and other inventors.

(5) Logical reasoning, both deductive and inductive, including analysis and synthesis. Every academic subject is based upon its own logic or discipline; each study begins with certain basic assumptions or axioms out of which are built, by logical processes, the contents of the course. Mathematics is a lan-

guage of logical thinking, using symbols and numbers instead of words. It is in the social sciences that we need especially to remember the requirements of logical reasoning, to protect us from false propaganda and demagoguery; but here such reasoning is hardest to apply, for human values cannot be reduced to syllogisms or mathematical equations. Every college graduate, however, should be able to detect obvious fallacies in reasoning, and to construct an argument that will withstand attack. For this reason, debate is one of the most rewarding of extracurricular activities.

(6) Judgment, which remains suspended until all the evidence is in, weighs it critically, recognizes absurdities and inadequacies, then finally evaluates fairly, without prejudice. All of us are inclined to "snap judgment," which is really pre-judice. If we feel free to pass judgment without knowledge, we lay ourselves open to the charge of insincerity, bigotry, or shallowness. Some courses in college, in all the fields, should be taught in such a way that issues are not decided by the instructor; but the student is asked to seek his own evidence and reach his own decision only after he has covered the field adequately. We are inclined to accept too much on the authority of others; someday we must be our own authority. The seminar course and the honors paper are excellent devices for producing this result.

(7) Creative imagination, which takes many diverse parts and molds them into a new unity. Modern education calls this integration, the attempt to perceive unity in the midst of diversity, to create order and beauty out of chaos. It is the ability to suggest new hypotheses which open up vast new avenues of thought. In science we find a Newton and a Darwin, in literature a Keats or a Tolstoi, in art a Michelangelo, in music a Beethoven, in religion, Jesus. The average man can share the possession of this greatest human power with the masters; all of us have within us some of the divine creative urge. In the

cultivation of creative power lies the greatest joy of the teacher, and the greatest hope for a better world.

These seven functions of the mind are not performed in a vacuum. The mind concentrates on a specific problem, observes an event, remembers a phrase, associates persons and places, reasons about issues, judges values, and creates scientific hypotheses, religious doctrines, literature, and works of art. These functions are carried on under a wide variety of circumstances and for the realization of many different ends. For the proper exercise of some of them many techniques are required involving manual dexterity. Often, as in playing a musical instrument, one cannot begin using his mind until the technical difficulties are overcome. Playing the piano or the violin, as much as stenography or typing, is a manual as well as a mental achievement. Therefore, liberal education must not leave the hands untrained, nor frown upon this as vocational education.

Manual dexterity is largely a matter of habit—the initiation by the instructor of operative manipulations until the pupil can perform similarly and easily. In this way the student achieves an understanding of good workmanship, an important accomplishment of maturity. Good work is something that can and must be judged objectively; in engineering, the construction of a building is good, mediocre, or bad; no one will say, "Considering the fact that the architect and engineer have low I.Q.'s, this is a remarkably good building, and therefore we will rate it as class A." In the science laboratory, the worker has a good or a bad technique; if his manual dexterity cannot be brought to a high level, he will probably never succeed as a surgeon or dentist. Although many college students are looking toward careers in which manual labor plays a small part, it is difficult to imagine a full life in which artistic skill or laboratory technique or mechanical facility will not be useful.

Manual facility is the handmaid of experiment, through whose many forms in chemistry, physics, zoology, botany, geology, astronomy, and psychology man learns the nature of the physical universe and his own nature, the ways of testing their powers, and the means of controlling their actions. Medicine, engineering, and agriculture rest upon the basic art of experiment. In the development of a mature personality there must be contact with the scientific method, actual laboratory experience. Why must the student hold the test tube in his own hand? Can't he watch the professor demonstrate the experiment and thus learn its principles? The principles, perhaps; but not the art. The laboratory enables the student to participate in the miracle of creation by combining elements into compounds or generating electrical current; in this manner he is liberated from the primitive and childhood fears of the unknown forces of the physical world. Laboratory work is admittedly expensive and enormously time-consuming, but it is the only way to the mastery of force and matter.

Man matures not only in himself and through his physical activities and the handling of tools, but also in his relations with other human beings; he is a member of society. Can education make him a better, more poised, and adaptable social being? Some cynic might suggest that, if this is our aim, membership in a good country club would be more effective than experience at college. Society begins with the home. When is a man or woman a better member of his home? One answer might well be, when he appreciates it is an institution basic to our social structure (something he might learn through sociology), and especially when he understands what real homemaking involves.

An engineer can build a house, an interior decorator might be able to furnish it, or a home economist to cook a meal in it, but homemaking, in the sense of surrounding ourselves with a congenial environment enriched with books, art, music, and satisfying companionship, is a liberal art. Are colleges contributing something valuable to the home life of their graduates? The outsider is inclined to poke fun at college courses in "Marriage and the Family," but the significant fact is that marriages which grew out of campus romances have a much lower percentage of divorce and separation than those without this bond. Our curricula and our college social programs must be constructed upon the assumption that education can bring out latent social abilities, and control those who are too aggressively extrovert.

Outside the home lies the neighborhood, of which man becomes a better member when he enjoys a rich and varied social life and conducts himself courteously and co-operatively. This comes only from living in that kind of atmosphere, the environment which the best colleges attempt to provide for their students. Social adaptability is perhaps taught in the dormitory, the dining room, the college dance, the student union, dramatics, the glee club, and other activities rather than in the formal course; but the important fact is that it can be taught, and is therefore a legitimate function of the college. Some people object to the large share of time such features demand in a college course; but these same critics will recognize and praise the qualities produced when they see them revealed in a socially mature man or woman. Education should not apologize for social niceties; it should rather study to see how it may better prepare students for considerate and gracious living.

The problem of personal adjustment is not merely a matter of the home and the drawing room; it is also a concern of the business office. Better workers need more than mere manual dexterity; they need to be well adjusted vocationally. This requires expert guidance in college to see that the students' abilities, interests, handicaps, and needs are considered when the vocation is chosen. Managerial positions require ability to handle personnel effectively and sympathetically; this can be taught and built into the personality of the prospective manager.

Beyond the neighborhood stretches the city, the state, the nation, the world, the whole framework that binds together the human family. Can education make better citizens? A man becomes a better citizen when he understands democratic social processes and seeks to bring them about. The most effective way for America to combat communism and fascism and every other foreign ism is not to bar them from our campuses by gag laws or teachers' oaths, but to demonstrate how the material and spiritual ends of human life can be attained more fully by the intelligent and unselfish co-operation of free individuals than by the coercion of state power. A liberally educated citizen is sensitive to the rights of his neighbor and the area of neighborhood has no political or geographical boundaries. He respects the opinions of others, for he realizes that there can be no democracy without civil liberties—free speech, free press, free worship, free courts, free vote, and minority rights. If in college he is reared in an atmosphere of free exchange of opinion, of debate and query, he is likely to agree with the sentiment attributed to Voltaire that, though he disapproves of what his neighbor says, he will defend to the death his neighbor's right to say it. Graduates of liberal arts colleges are not likely to be radicals or reactionaries, but, as the name implies, liberals. As such, they learn to defend themselves against misleading propaganda, to call for justice, to appeal to reason. The educated mind seeks the facts so that it can reach its own conclusions; it abhors all violence.

The realm of the good citizen is not limited to political action. In matters of health, he is interested not only in his own physical welfare, but also in protecting the lives of others, through control of disease, community hygiene, and general improvement of the public health. He conserves our natural resources, knowing that generations are to come who will need these forests, coal beds, oil fields, gas wells, and soil. He studies physics and chemistry, geology and botany, not merely to become a laboratory technician but to make intelligent use of the services and products of these sciences.

Undoubtedly education can influence students toward an understanding of world affairs, and thus prevent their becoming provincial or chauvinistic in their Americanism; the problems of Europe, Asia, Africa, Australia, South America, Mexico, and Canada are part of the responsibility of a liberally educated American citizen. The social sciences of history, economics, sociology, and government have as their common aim the study of human actions, interactions, and institutions, for the purpose of freeing man from his fear of other men, largely induced by ignorance. We profit all too little from the experience of our forebears, make exactly the same mistakes they made, and turn our knowledge of human frailty into a weapon to destroy ourselves. Nevertheless, the possibility of profiting by experience is there and it is to be hoped that future generations will learn how to use it better.

CHAPTER V

General Education and Liberal Education

There exists considerable confusion in the mind of the average educator, student, and general reader between the terms "general education" and "liberal education." This confusion has probably arisen because what is today called "general education" was for centuries considered a part of liberal education, and the distinction is a matter of recent development. The confusion has been increased by the careless manner in which educational pronouncements have referred to general education as "that education which is usually completed within the junior college, or within the first two years of a four-year college." Although some institutions may make a distinction on the basis of the time when each is emphasized, this is a distinction without a real difference, and does not describe the purposes or qualities of either type. General education should not be thought of as limited to the period of primary and secondary education; there is general education upon the level of maturity which is definitely not that of childhood or adolescence.

General education, as its name implies, is the education common to our "genus," or kind, the education needed to enable an individual to become an intelligent and co-operative member of society rather than that designed to bring out the distinctive features of his own personality. If an individual is to become an effective member of the group in which he lives he must first of all gain a mastery of the tools needed to share fully in the common life: manual dexterity, self-expression through speech and writing, the ability to read with understanding, the ready use of numbers and mathematical methods, and psychology for self-analysis and self-realization. The need of manual training for maturity we have already discussed, and the laboratory course in science, art, music, and other fields as an excellent way to provide it. Knowledge of English, our "mother tongue," is so clearly necessary that some formal requirement is found in practically every college. However, very few have succeeded in devising any scheme of instruction that accomplishes the ends desired. As a result, a high percentage of our college graduates are unable to speak effectively to an audience, to write their findings or ideas with clarity and force, or to read with pleasure anything more complicated than the daily newspaper or a mystery thriller.

The level of achievement that should be demanded of all students in this area should be. high, and the requirements should be continued in some form throughout the college period. Regardless of the final vocational choice a student may make, he will be seriously handicapped if his English is faulty. For many students, the study of a foreign language can be of immense help is understanding English grammar, increasing vocabulary, and achieving a "language sense." How much mathematics is needed for general education is a debatable issue, but certainly all arithmetical processes, the concrete space relationships of geometry, and abstractions of algebra enter into the daily life of practically every educated person. The place of psychology is unsettled; some insist that it is a natural science, others that it is a social science. In the area of general education, however, its greatest usefulness is as a tool to the understanding of ourselves, our minds, our motives, our actions, to help us control these more effectively.

But man does not live in isolation; he is part of a human society, which he must understand if he is to relate himself effectively to it. Beyond the family lies the neighborhood, and then in widening circles the city, the state, the nation, and the world. The study of these relations is the function of the social sciences—economics, government, sociology, religion, education, anthropology, geography—which broaden our general education to the point that we feel at home among the members and the institutions of our complex society. Not that it is necessary for the student to learn all the laws of economics, the history of economic theory, the principles of business administration, money, banking, labor, and the score or more other special twigs of this branch of learning—those are subject matter for specialists. On the level of general education, all that is necessary is that the student become familiar with two or three of the major problems of our economic order—perhaps prices or corporations or taxation—and understand the methods used by social scientists in attacking these problems. Also, it should be made clear that such a problem as labor or crime is not the concern merely of the economist or the sociologist, but also of the educator, the political scientist, the psychologist, and the religious leader, all of whom have different approaches to the same problem. The foreign languages become tools for studying international relations, mathematics provides social statistics, and thus tool subjects become integrated with the content.

Natural science provides a third side to our general education frame of reference. Above us shine the sun and moon and stars, described by astronomy; the forces of our universe, its energy in various forms, are codified by physics. Beneath our feet lies the earth, whose secrets come to light under the scrutiny of geology and geography; within and around us is life, both plant and animal, the field of botany and zoology and physiology. And all matter, whether earth or plant or animal, is reduced to its elements and studied in the test tube of chemistry. Here, again, it is not the education of the future chemist or electrical engineer that is needed for general education, but the spirit of the amateur in science; we must achieve enough knowledge of appearances and principles and laws to make us feel at ease in the physical universe.

Man lives, however, not merely in himself, in society, and in the physical world, but also in the stream of time, the fourth side of general education. Behind the present individual stretch thousands of years of recorded history, masterpieces of artistic, musical, and literary achievement, and the philosophical and religious ideas of billions of ancestors. Before him lies the unknown future, a tremendous challenge to his thought. No individual can hope to become acquainted with his entire human heritage; even the greatest historians can achieve that for only a small segment of time or territory. But the function of the humanities, the study of our human inheritance, is to show the student some of the noblest attempts of man to discover and create experiences and objects which have more than material value and to help him understand the meaning of human life in terms of its aspirations and ideals. Whereas the sciences seek to discover, describe, analyze, and clarify facts, the humanities seek to appraise, judge, and criticize values. Science asks, Is it true or false? The humanities demand, Is it good or bad? All men need some training in answering both questions.

Upon this four-sided frame of general education, liberal education, the unique patternmaker, will select the threads and weave the manifold permutations and combinations that constitute personality. Henry James wrote one of his most brilliant short stories with the title "The Figure in the Carpet," the plot dealing with the unsuccessful efforts of literary critics to discover what the secret of the individual style of a great novelist actually was; the tragedy of much of our education today lies in the failure of educators to develop a significant "figure in the carpet" of their students. This truly liberal education is much more difficult than general education to teach and to attain, for it places greater emphasis upon the higher mental powers. The facts and values of general education can be assimilated by the mind of the student chiefly through observation, association, or memory; they can be tested objectively. But liberal education demands logical reasoning and creative imagination; these cannot be absorbed by mere contact, but must grow within the mind; imagination is too unstandardized to be tested on a Hollorith machine. An artist may learn to use his tools correctly, but the picture he creates is not a function of his tools, but of his artistic imagination, his individuality as an artist. A college can insist, as part of its general education requirement, that every student be able to write correct and clear English, but poetry, the short story, creative literature in general, are a product of liberal education, possible only for the gifted and trained individual.

Liberal education is so called because it liberates man from the confinements of mind-slavery, and opens to him the heritage of the "liberi," or free men. In Periclean Athens or medieval society this meant the privileges of the nobility, the thin upper layer of society; in American democracy it must mean opportunities for all citizens to realize fully their potentialities. Biology has taught us that every specimen is unique, that although the elements, the general pattern, and the central core may be alike, each flower, bird, and human being has some feature, or combination of features, which sets him apart from his fellows. In like manner, among human beings, the psychological patterns, or "profiles," are as individualized as our thumbprints. Given a hundred or more personality variables, the number of permutations and combinations approaches infinity, like the possible patterns in an Oriental rug. In the rug, the frame upon which it is woven (general education) may be the same as that used for a hundred others, the wool or silk may be similar, but the glory of the true Oriental lies in its individuality of pattern. So with man; his frame and flesh, his muscles and organs, may be like those of others, but the pattern of his personality, his temper and spirit, are unique and peculiarly his own.

It is, therefore, the function of liberal education to use every device at its command to understand and develop this uniqueness. Only by recognizing the strong elements, the gifts or talents, and by encouraging their development can a teacher help the student gain full possession of his powers; only by finding the gaps and weaknesses and correcting them can education prevent failure. The choices of the student must be wisely guided, if the over-all pattern of personality is to have symmetry and beauty. If it is to avoid being haphazard, amorphous, and disjointed, it must possess harmony and must hang together. Its parts must be intimately related; there must be no separation of the individual, his tools, his universe, his society, his time, and his art. In the developed ability to perceive these relationships lies wisdom as contrasted with mere information. In the medieval cathedral was reflected the entire life of a people: Chartres illuminates the history and economy and art of the Middle Ages and shows forth the abiding faith of the Christian Church. Liberally educated persons should become an equally integrated reflection of the best that is within themselves and the civilization of which they are a part. The Greeks had a motto: "Man is the measure of all things"; certainly the resultant man is the measure of liberal education.

Our lives as individuals begin simultaneously with our lives as members of the human race. Liberal education, therefore, must begin as soon as general education, and both must continue throughout life. Although the former is built upon the latter, it is not necessary for general education to be completed before liberal education is started. The two are complementary, not competitive; general education begins as the dominant part, but gradually occupies less and less of the time of the student, as liberal education gradually expands. Liberal education is no abstract concept, dwelling in the brains of educational philosophers. It signifies the processes by which the mind frees itself from instinctive behavior, from ignorance and bigotry, and learns to function objectively and disinterestedly.

The old "three R's" of readin', 'ritin', and 'rithmetic are still

an excellent program of fundamentals for elementary education
and much of secondary and college general education. But for
truly liberal education, perhaps we need a new three R's—
Reason in the field of ideas, Resourcefulness in contacts with
the physical universe, Responsibility toward society. By the
first is meant not merely formal logic, but the broad perspective
that understanding gives, the sense of proportion that marks
the truly wise man. Resourcefulness must mean more than
manual facility; it implies the flexibility and adaptability and
inventiveness of both body and mind. Responsibility does more
than accept the duties thrust upon it by society, it freely assumes burdens which it could avoid; it seeks leadership not for
selfish ends, but as a larger service to the common weal. Given
these broad interpretations, Reason, Resourcefulness, and Responsibility may well be considered the distinctive attributes
of the liberally educated man.

The young man or woman eager for financial success in life
often asks, "But what kind of job or profession does a liberal
education prepare me to enter? Can I step from the liberal arts
college into a position with a future?" The answer can be made
that liberal education prepares for all occupations, and gives
special training for those which emphasize the higher mental
activities. For some, such as teaching, writing, journalism,
music, art, and most fields of business, a judiciously organized
program of studies in the liberal arts might well provide all the
specific education required for success. For others, such as
scientific research, college teaching, and personnel management, the graduate schools of arts and sciences provide from
one to three years of additional instruction. For the professions
and near professions, such as medicine, dentistry, law, the
ministry, engineering, nursing, business administration, social
service, and the higher journalism, there are professional
schools, usually requiring a considerable period of general and
liberal education on the college level before admission. The

Association of American Medical Colleges has gone on record as being opposed to "premedical" and strongly in favor of good basic education: "Intellect and intelligence, the power to understand and to reason; above all, the ability or power to think." Similar stands have been taken by schools of law, theology, business administration, and other professions. A student trained to think, to reason, and to be resourceful and responsible in his undergraduate college will naturally be a leader in the professional school, and will advance more rapidly upon entering the profession itself.

The student who is considering his career must look at it as a whole, not merely in its immediate possibilities. There are undoubtedly shortcuts to positions which pay good salaries; the Abraham Lincolns, Henry Fords, and Thomas Edisons will get to the top without any formal education. But the experience of mankind shows that those with the complete and thorough background of general and liberal education and professional training will eventually pull ahead of their rivals. The man who attains success with a minimum of preparation would in most cases have been even more successful with more education. Also, it is worth considering that financial success is not the whole basis for judging the value of a life; the richness of man's inner thoughts and social attitudes can be a "never failing treasury filled with boundless stores of grace."

The normal order of development, therefore, should be general education first, to make man feel at home in the physical, social, and intellectual world; then liberal education, to bring out the pattern of his individuality, to prepare him for responsible leadership; and finally specialized or professional education, to induce the skills by which he can make a living. But general education should never stop; like a growing circle, its circumference should always touch on new areas of the unknown which need exploration. Also, liberal and specialized education can reach down into the early years, beginning as an awakening interest and gradually growing into a true vocation, or "calling," which unites all the strands of understanding the world and making a living into making a complete and rewarding life.

CHAPTER VI

Curricula as Means to Education

Although the aims and processes of general education and liberal education have undergone careful examination and been the subject of searching criticism during the past twenty-five years, actual changes in curricular practices have come slowly. Only an occasional institution here and there has been bold enough to break away from the prevailing pattern of the nine-month year, one hundred twenty semester hours of credit, certain required elementary departmental courses, plus a major in a single department. New institutions like Bennington College, and even firmly established ones like the University of Chicago or the University of Minnesota, which have ventured upon new programs, have not greatly influenced the national situation. It will be interesting to note the changes that will take place now that Harvard, Yale, Amherst, and other well-established "conservative" colleges have given the hallmark of their approval to the broader aspects of general education. Perhaps in ten years the prevailing pattern will have changed materially, but for the present, in respect to methods of instruction and the specific requirements for receiving the degree, ninety per cent of the colleges of America follow a pattern which has changed little in over twenty-five years.

The statement of the purposes of a college are usually indicated in ideal terms in the annual catalogue. Such statements mean little unless they are implemented by the entrance and graduation requirements, by the course offerings, and by the teaching methods actually prevailing in the institution; there is too often considerable discrepancy between the professed

53

purposes and the practice. However, for such a general view of curricular practices as this chapter represents, we have felt justified in accepting catalogue announcements as our chief source of information. A careful examination of more than one hundred fifty catalogues, representing most of the oldest, wealthiest, and most highly respected institutions, as well as some of the younger, struggling, avowedly experimental ones, gives us a picture of the prevalent American pattern, plus some of the interesting variations which are now being tried, and which may point the way to accepted practices of the future.

By 1890 the college calendar had been established with nearly fixed dates determined by the needs of an agricultural population. Because summer was the season when workers were needed in the fields, the schools, elementary and secondary, were open only during the late fall, winter, and early spring months, and the colleges followed their example. The average college year began around the fifteenth of September, commencement came on the fifteenth of June; in the larger colleges and universities, and especially in the teachers' colleges, there was an abbreviated summer session, usually of six or eight weeks, designed especially for public school teachers who were working toward their degrees.

The first break in this uniformity of calendar came with the introduction by the University of Chicago of the quarter system, which placed the summer session upon an equal basis with the other quarters of the year, and gave the student the privilege of accelerating his program by attending all four quarters or of taking his vacation in the winter if he desired. Bennington College, being in the grip of Vermont winters, and being attended by many young women (and faculty) who preferred to spend their winters in a warmer climate, went to the logical plan of arranging their college year to run September through December, and then April through July. In addition to the studies of the regular terms, they arranged a serious study or work projects to be pursued during the winter months while the student was away from the campus.

The Second World War, with its overlapping civilian, army, and navy schedules, forced many changes in the college calendar. Many institutions went on a "trimester" scheme, with terms beginning in March, July, and November. Others found themselves starting new programs every few weeks. Now that these programs are concluded, the colleges have an opportunity to think through the whole problem of the "academic year." For a few years, the influx of veterans anxious to make up for lost time may force a twelve-month schedule on colleges desiring to serve this group, but eventually it will be possible to revert to the old familiar nine months. When that day arrives, will colleges seek to fit their schedules to the local climate, the needs of the students, and the desires of the faculty, or will they wait for the public schools to make a change?

Some college teachers will tell you that they chose teaching rather than a higher salaried position in industry because of the long summer vacations; perhaps the programs of our northern colleges could be made even more attractive if the vacations were in the winter. Summer study in Maine or Wisconsin or Washington could conceivably be the most effective of the year. Some preparatory schools have their "winter campuses" in the South; the heavy investment in plants and equipment makes such a scheme impracticable for colleges and universities. It is clear, however, that America has advanced so far beyond the agricultural stage that seasons of crop cultivation should not determine the dates for the opening and closing of colleges; other more relevant influences should mold the pattern. Also, other than the convenience of the occasional student who wishes to transfer from one institution to another, it is hard to find a good reason why all the colleges of the country should follow the same plan. Here, as well as in other areas, individuality should be possible.

In the development of the courses of study within the college years, standardization has again been the paramount force. Various standardizing organizations, such as state boards of education and regional associations, have helped to bring this about, even though they may now be broadening their requirements and urging colleges to develop individual programs. In the search for uniform standards, colleges for the most part have used as measures either the amount of credits accumulated or the amount of knowledge assimilated or the amount of time spent. Almost all the catalogues examined in this study state the requirements for graduation in terms of credits—one hundred twenty semester hours plus physical education, or fifteen to twenty "year courses" as an alternative statement of the same thing.

Colleges on the quarter system merely translate these figures into one hundred eighty quarter hours, or forty-odd quarter courses; the method is the same. We are reminded of the penny bank; when the student has put in the proper number of credits and had them duly registered on the college machine, the bank opens up automatically and presents him with a diploma. The method can be defended as a guardian of the degree against "short-cut" frauds, and it can probably be said that if a student accumulates one hundred twenty semester hours with passing grades he will certainly have attended thousands of class meetings under dozens of instructors, and must have profited somewhat thereby. But it can hardly satisfy anyone who wants to feel confident that the college graduate is an educated person.

A few colleges, wanting to give added significance to their degrees, require the passing of a series of examinations, fitted to the various levels of general education and departmental specialization. The degree will be granted when the student gives evidence that he has acquired sufficient knowledge. It is argued that this device makes the instructor and the student "partners" in preparing to meet the examiners; the student will realize that the teacher is there to help him, and not to inflict punishment upon him or even to decide whether he passes or fails—therefore, there will be "bon rapport" among all concerned. It is conceivable, however, that if the student thinks of a college as an examination bureau accompanied by several "cramming schools" he will receive little true education from the college during the period of time he is there. If his chief purpose is to pass the examinations and secure the degree, he may concentrate upon the devices for accomplishing this, and miss much of the enrichment of living and maturing of personality that should result from attending college.

Several other institutions, not content with credits or examinations as evidence that a student has achieved the full purpose of their programs or reached the level of maturity they covet for their graduates, have standardized the time requirement by specifying four years of college residence as a condition for their degree. The philosophy of the residence requirement has been well expressed by Northwestern University in its statement of new requirements for the B.A. degree: "The program is planned as a four-year program with no summer class work . . . Minds educated to solve problems and so cultivated as to enrich one's personal life are not the products of a hurried learning. The whole purpose of this program is to deepen the educational experience. To accomplish this end an extensive period is essential that the student may have time to reflect on his experience and to mature his ideas . . . The Program fosters in the student's mind the conviction that an education is a long-term process rather than a matter of passing separate courses or accumulating credits."

The four-year residence requirement is based on a frank recognition that the degree does not mean the same level of attainment in the case of any two students who secure it, and that the real question is not whether one student can reach as high a level in two or three years as some other student in four, but can any student build as broad and firm a foundation of education in three years as the same student could do in four. There is no question that college students, even after going through the winnowing processes involved in college entrance, vary greatly in their intellectual and moral capacities. Among the varied gifts possessed by students is the capacity to work rapidly. The time factor is an important element of difference in the performances of different minds.

The mind that moves most rapidly is not necessarily the one which gains the deepest insight into the problems with which it deals. Often a slow-moving mind is characterized by an awareness of relationships between situations resulting in truer insights, better balanced judgments, and ultimately in surer wisdom, than are gained by more agile and quicker minds which are also likely to be more superficial. No combination of mental characteristics in any particular student seems to make it obvious that his training at the undergraduate level should be accomplished in less time than is required to enable the college to carry on a program that will bring the richest opportunities to all its students.

A student who accelerates his program in an institution organized on a four-year basis finds himself out of step with much of the valuable routine of the institution and is likely to miss many of its intangible values, often to be found in the incidental phases of its life. The presence of such students tends to weaken the faith of the other students in their programs and to lower the morale of the whole institution. A student entering such an institution should consider it from the beginning as a four-year experience, and not plan to withdraw after one or two years to enter another institution. This all-too-common procedure is unfair to both colleges, the one entered as well as the one left, and is likely to react unfavorably upon the whole educational development of the individual student. Colleges which emphasize the four-year residence requirement also discourage their students from transferring at the end of two or three years to a professional school and then expecting the college to grant them a bachelor's degree after two years of professional training—a practice long encouraged by most professional schools but now coming to be discouraged by some of the stronger ones which desire to admit only those who have had the highest type of undergraduate training.

In addition to quantity requirements, whether measured by credits, areas covered by examination, or by time spent in residence, most colleges have adopted requirements seeking to place emphasis upon quality. In many institutions this emphasis is sought for through the "point system"; every grade received in a course has a point value from plus 5 down to minus 2, and the student expecting to be graduated must accumulate at least as many "grade points" as he does credits. Some institutions state the requirement in terms of the general average (usually C), others in the number of hours or courses with C grades or better, but the general result is the same. Ohio State and St. Louis universities place a higher requirement on courses counted toward the "major" than on those outside. The University of Minnesota and Washington and Lee place a premium on high-quality work by making it possible for the good students to reduce the number of credit hours required for graduation by securing surplus quality points. Such mechanical devices are rejected by the most lively experimenters among the women's colleges, Bennington and Sarah Lawrence.

At these institutions no credits are recorded, and, as the Bennington bulletin states it, "The standard of accomplishment is determined for each student both in terms of her own best effort and in relation to the accomplishment of a successful worker in the field. Descriptive reports are made by her instructors twice each semester, and the gist of these reports is given the student by her counselor. Once a year the student's whole record is summarized in a letter . . . No final comprehensive examinations are given. The student's whole accomplishment is considered in recommending her for the degree." The Sarah Lawrence plan is similar, placing emphasis upon the evaluation of the needs, abilities, and interests of each student, and then setting the goals to fit.

The foregoing suggests that our colleges might well adopt a new composite standard of time, plus credits, plus quality, for graduation or "promotion" from year to year, all adjusted to fit the innate mental ability of the student, the rate at which he works, and the goal he has in view. This requires, of course, a careful examination and diagnosis of each student upon entrance, careful counseling by a competent staff, frequent retests and readjustments of goals, and a re-examination at the conclusion to see what growth has taken place. Of course, such an individualized, or "tailor-made," program costs more than machine methods, but in the manufacture of a delicate and tremendously precious individuality which is expected to stay in running order for fifty years or more, the added expense represents a good investment if thereby the potentialities of the student are more fully developed.

Any discussion of time and course credits leads directly to the problem of the normal working load of the college student. Labor unions have agitated for a forty-hour working week, but the program of no serious student can be confined within any such limit. Let us assume that physical education and extra-curricular activities should not be considered as work—and those who have run the school paper or acted in a play or played on the football team might challenge this—then the academic or course-work program might be expected to occupy about forty-five hours each week, with fifteen hours in the classroom and "two hours of preparation for each hour in class." The two-hour preparation formula is, however, unfair to the poor student, and gives the good student an excuse for loafing if he finishes the two-hour assignment in thirty minutes.

Therefore, the instructor might well say to his class: "As one of your five courses, this is entitled to nine hours of your time. Three hours will be spent in the classroom, and the other six hours in preparation [or perhaps some in the laboratory]. I have the list of the members of the class, with the 'adjustment factor on working ability' for each one of you. Some of you have brilliant minds, work and read rapidly, and are planning to major in this department; therefore your assignments will be considerably longer and more difficult than those given to the slower students or those who are taking this course for its general educational value." This individualization will require more of an instructor's time and his teaching load should be correspondingly reduced. Here, again, the extra expense will be justified if the plan encourages students to work up closer to the limits of their abilities. Also, there is nothing wrong with the practice of awarding prizes as inducements to students to do more than the minimum required to pass the course—cash, medals, prize scholarships and fellowships, Phi Beta Kappa keys. The English universities have long differentiated between honors and pass degrees, and this practice might well receive greater emphasis in America.

Turning now to the actual programs offered, it is safe to assume that in the great majority of colleges heaviest stress during the first two years will be laid upon general education. The pattern for accomplishing this, however, is strongly affected by the organization of the college and by the goals that an institution may specify as representing the objective of its program. Many universities and some colleges, for example, Allegheny, Bucknell, Colorado College, Goucher, Grinnell, Rollins, Redlands, and Washington and Jefferson, have set this period aside in a junior college, with separate administration and frequently separate faculty; examinations or the accumulation of sixty semester hours and sixty quality points are usually required for the student to leave the lower division. Elsewhere the departmental organization is dominant; the larger the faculty, the more departments there are and the more elementary courses are being offered; therefore, the more "logrolling" is required to achieve a general education curriculum. A more recent and flexible development is the "divisional" organization, whereby the departments are combined into humanities, social studies, and sciences, and the student is permitted to choose any course within the division. These three areas are the most popular divisional organizations, but there are other combinations in operation. For example, the course requirements at Oberlin are based upon the following carefully reasoned pattern:

1. In a universe built up of like materials, which undergo like changes under like conditions, upon a tiny changing planet,   THE PHYSICAL SCIENCES

2. Many forms of life have evolved, including man.   THE BIOLOGICAL SCIENCES

3. Man possesses a complex and highly integrated organization: PSYCHOLOGY

4. Living in society with other men, he tries to understand group life, to adapt himself to it, and to mold it to his needs;   THE SOCIAL SCIENCES

5. He has achieved effective forms of thought and of the communication of thought;   LANGUAGES, MATHEMATICS, LOGIC

6. He learns to enjoy the beautiful and, so far as he can, to create the beautiful; and   LITERATURE, THE FINE ARTS, MUSIC

7. He strives to understand the sum total of life, and to live with reference thereto.   PHILOSOPHY, RELIGION

The requirements at Oberlin for "distribution" of studies are based upon these seven areas, at least one course being required in each. Goucher specifies eight "desirable ends of education" as follows: (1) to establish and maintain physical and mental health; (2) to comprehend and communicate ideas both in English and in foreign languages; (3) to understand the scientific method in theory and application; (4) to understand the heritage of the past in its relation to the present; (5) to establish satisfying relations with individuals and with groups; (6) to utilize resources with economic and aesthetic satisfaction; (7) to enjoy literature and the other arts; (8) to appreciate religious and philosophical values. Reasonable progress toward the attainment of these ends is required of all students, but each student is given freedom under the guidance of professionally trained personnel officers to choose such courses of study in meeting these ends as she believes will best meet her needs.

A committee of the American Council on Education, working with the educational branches of the Army and Navy to set up a pattern of general education valuable for members of the armed forces, suggested fifteen courses, not all of equal weight or length, which will be suggestive to colleges seeking a pattern of their own: (1) Personal and Community Health; (2) Oral and Written Communication; (3) Problems of Social Adjustment; (4) Marriage and Family Adjustment; (5) Development of American Thought and Institutions; (6) Problems of American Life; (7) America in International Affairs; (8) Biological Science; (9) Physical Science; (10) American Life and Ideals in Literature; (11) Readings in the Short Story, Drama, Biography, Poetry, and Novel; (12) Form and Function of Art in Society; (13) Music in Relation to Human Experience; (14) Philosophy and Religion—the Meaning and Value of Life; and (15) Vocational Orientation.

However, in most colleges and universities the requirements are stated by departments or groups of departments. English, especially the course in freshman composition, is almost a universal "must," and it is usually followed by a required course in literature, taught by the English department. Occasionally work in speech is included in this English course, but the separation between these two departments has been so marked that the combined course is the exception. At some colleges, among them Amherst, Berea, Creighton, Hamilton, Iowa, Marquette, and Wellesley, the speech department has been strong enough to insist upon a specific requirement. Obviously, all aspects of communication skills are greatly needed, and it is difficult to understand why oral composition is so often neglected. Some institutions state the requirement of written English in terms of ability, and insist that a student pass a proficiency examination; Allegheny, California, Columbia, Drew, Emory, George Washington, Harvard, Kenyon, Muskingum, and Ohio State allow the student to take this examination at entrance, and excuse him from further work if he shows the required proficiency. Ohio State even grants course credits toward graduation for passing such entrance examinations.

Next to English in percentage of frequency is the foreign-language requirement; less than ten per cent have no such requirement. Here, again, there is a struggle between the entrenched departments and newcomers. In the Catholic colleges and some of the more conservative eastern colleges, the requirement of Latin or Greek still holds for the A.B. degree, though we occasionally find the odd choice, "Latin or Greek or Mathematics." French, German, and Spanish hold the center of the stage, but the war has pushed toward Italian, Portuguese, Russian, Chinese and Japanese, and we occasionally find the national influence, as in the Polish courses at DePaul and the Norwegian at St. Olaf. Science departments urge their majors to study German as the key to scientific publications; other departments have their individual preferences—Business wants Spanish, Law places Latin first, Religion advises Greek, Literature likes French, and International Relations stresses Russian.

The requirement is customarily stated in terms of hours or courses, frequently allowing high school study to fulfill part of the total; usually the second-year level will satisfy the faculty, but Butler, Drew, Richmond, Tulane, Wabash, and others demand additional courses. A score or more state this requirement in terms of reading knowledge, and allow it to be satisfied by the passing of an examination. Foreign-language instruction in American colleges and universities probably falls short of its professed objectives by a wider margin than is true in any other area of curricular offerings. Other departments rarely, if ever, make use of foreign languages in their work, with the result that accomplishment in this field fails to have any function and the student acquires no real facility in reading or speaking. It is here that we have learned most from war training programs and it is to be hoped that this experience will have permanent results in improving the effectiveness of language instruction throughout the country so that American students may gain a more practical mastery of the languages of their neighbors.

The sciences, with reasonable choice between physics, chemistry, and biology, and with occasional permission of geology or psychology, are customarily required for at least one year, the emphasis being placed upon a "laboratory science." Perhaps one in five colleges demands more than one science, but usually the second science can be replaced by mathematics. A mathematics requirement as such is held to by Antioch, Creighton, DePaul, Emory, Union, Vanderbilt, and Virginia, but in most curricula it is included as one of the science group.

If any one of the social sciences is required, it is usually history, but the student is customarily given a choice of any department for one year. Religion, at times grouped with the social studies, becomes a specific departmental requirement in most of the church-controlled institutions; the Catholic colleges often require courses in religion during all four years. Philosophy and/or psychology form a required group at Albion, Bryn Mawr, Cornell, DePauw, Peabody, Haverford, Spelman, Wells, and others.

Physical education in some form is required in practically

every college in America; formerly the requirement ran for the first two years only, but the war has spread it temporarily over the whole period and opened up the problem for further consideration. At Barnard, Bowdoin, Bucknell, Cornell, North Carolina, and others, this is combined during the freshman year with a required course on hygiene.

These, then, are the most frequently repeated departmental "musts." Only a few, among them Allegheny, Carnegie Tech, Chicago, Colgate, Columbia, and Knox, have gone the entire distance away from the strictly departmental courses and set up special "general education" courses cutting across departmental lines. Knox's required freshman course in "The Middle West" was a good example of this, for it required the participation of fourteen departments representing all the divisions, and secured intensity by limiting its area to the eight states of Ohio, Michigan, Indiana, Illinois, Missouri, Iowa, Wisconsin, and Minnesota. Out of this course have now grown three "integrated general education" courses in literature-arts, social studies, and science, which are administered entirely outside the dominion of any department.

In no one of the three courses is any attempt made to cover all the topics that would be treated in the separate departmental freshman courses, but a limited number of topics best suited to general education are chosen from the division; for example, the literature-arts course is organized around three concepts—the vocabulary and techniques of the arts, the relation of the arts to the personalities of the artists, and the relation of arts to society; in the science course, astronomy, geology, physics, chemistry, zoology, botany, and physiology are drawn upon, but each for only from three to ten problems or topics which yield to scientific treatment and reveal the scientific method.

The foregoing patterns of general education are today undergoing important changes, but the idea and conviction of the necessity of general education have become thoroughly entrenched, as recent reports from Harvard, Columbia, Yale, Amherst, Iowa, Northwestern, and many others reveal. After the student has achieved a reasonable foundation by taking several "distributed" or "interrelated" courses on a fairly elementary level, and after he has either accumulated sufficient credit hours or passed the proper number of qualifying examinations, he is ready for advanced study. On the upper level the work is usually carried on in a field or department of specialization, called a "major," of usually twenty-four semester hours, plus a "minor" of twelve hours or more, and additional electives to make up the prescribed total.

Several colleges allow "area majors" in two or more departments, such as history and literature, or languages and international relations; Hamilton College insists upon two full majors; Washington University sets no major requirement, but insists that the student carry some advanced courses. To dissuade juniors and seniors from filling their programs with elementary courses, many colleges give only limited credit for freshman courses taken by seniors, and several have definite "upper level" course requirements; Columbia asks for sixty "maturity credits," Denver for twenty-five quarter hours in advanced courses, Lawrence for six advanced courses, Pomona for thirty-six hours above freshman level, and Ohio State for two-thirds of all the work taken in senior college.

Work in the later years is distinguished not only by its greater concentration and difficulty, but also by different methods of instruction. The advanced courses are usually given to smaller groups, and therefore the seminar procedure is possible. Albion, Oberlin, Scripps, and Swarthmore all emphasize the seminar method in the junior and senior years, and Hiram has adopted it as the basis through all four years of its "single course," or intensive study, program. The seminar abolishes the lecture by the instructor, and substitutes the round-table discussion of project reports prepared by individual students and presented orally to the class. It is individualized education, and therefore expensive, but possible in the average college. Developing alongside the seminar is the independent reading course, in which the student takes a list of books in a field, reads them at his own convenience, and reports upon them individually to the instructor. This device is so inexpensive that no college interested in individualization should be without it.

From the English universities, largely via Rhodes scholars, the plan of honors study came to America, where it has enjoyed a steady growth, so that at least thirty of the catalogues studied described well-developed schemes. Swarthmore is an excellent example of what can be done, with approximately half the students seeking an honors degree, devoting half their time during the last two years to this "graduate level" work. Reed, Washington and Lee, and others require a senior "thesis," but the honors method involves more than the mere preparation of a paper; it is individualized work at its best, and should be the goal of every liberal arts college student of ability.

The college of the future will probably require a final comprehensive examination in the field of the major before graduation, now required in several institutions where the honors plan has been established. Some are insisting upon both a written and an oral final, which is desirable when possible. The importance of this examination is variously estimated; some insist that the student who fails must take it again and postpone the date of graduation; others use it primarily to determine final graduation honors; a few grant course credit for passing it. The Graduate Record Examination of the Carnegie Foundation is used by several colleges for this purpose, and may become a standard device; it may, however, be supplemented by more localized and individualized testing devices.

The final development of individualization in education is tutorial instruction, the master-apprentice relationship, offered by Antioch, Harvard, Radcliffe, Rollins, Scripps, and Southwestern, among others, to juniors and seniors, and by Goucher, Knox, Sarah Lawrence, and others to freshmen. On the upper level, the device is not particularly new, since it has been employed in graduate instruction in the thesis course; the student merely works intimately with his major professor upon a topic closely related to his special interest. Goucher and Sarah Lawrence argue that freshmen need this individualized instruction more than do upperclassmen, because they are more confused and helpless and unmotivated than their elders.

A model tutorial program beginning with freshmen would be somewhat as follows: a sufficient number of faculty members, most of them full professors, are relieved of approximately one-third of their normal teaching load to devote themselves to tutorial instruction of freshmen, not more than twelve students being assigned to any one tutor. After a careful analysis of several diagnostic and achievement tests, the scores of which constitute the pattern of the student's "educational profile," or "psychograph," the tutor advises the student on his enrollment, and helps him plan his program of study. The tutorial "course" constitutes one-fourth of the student's entire freshman program and requires about ten hours of work each week. During the whole year the student meets twice weekly for personal conferences with his tutor, at which they discuss books assigned for reading, papers written by the student, the work being carried on in the other courses, techniques for remedying defects in the fundamental tools such as mathematics and English, and general personal and vocational problems. During the earlier years of college the student is expected to achieve reasonable skills in writing, mathematics, and a foreign language, demonstrated in a proficiency examination, and a general knowledge of literature and the arts, social studies and the sciences, to be tested in general education examinations.

The student can prepare for these tests in any of several

ways: (1) by superior high school work, which might enable him to pass all the proficiency examinations and one or more of the general education examinations on entrance, during the first week of college; (2) by enrolling in college courses designed to develop these skills, and in the special integrated general courses in these areas; (3) by enrolling in several departmental courses leading toward a major in one of the three divisions; (4) by private study with his tutor. Through this variety of choices the student can achieve as individualized a program of studies as he needs or desires.

The pressure of vocational preparation has been so great in recent years that many courses and subjects not traditionally considered "liberal" in nature have crept into the curriculum. None of these is actually required for the bachelor's degree, but in some colleges it is possible to receive an A.B. degree with a major in engineering or home economics or business administration. Many liberal arts colleges offer a professional degree in music—at Lawrence and Oberlin the "conservatory" is almost as large as the liberal arts college. Military science and naval science receive a large number of credit hours at all the ROTC institutions, and the number of these hours is likely to increase in the reorganization following the war. At least Albion, Antioch, Bates, Butler, and Colby offer five-year combined programs leading to a degree in nursing. Secretarial studies, commercial art, aeronautics, and library science all are given, though occasionally without credit. State laws concerning the preparation of high school teachers have practically compelled the colleges to credit professional training courses in educational methods and practice teaching toward the A.B. degree.

In this field of vocational preparation the influence of the larger universities upon the college is evident; in the universities it is possible for the student to take a program in the college of liberal arts and at the same time pursue some vocational courses; the independent, separately organized college is expected to offer no less. As to the wisdom of this policy, there are justifiably grave doubts, and the colleges would probably be happier if vocational courses could be eliminated. On the other hand, perhaps the teacher and the secretary and the businessman and the musician and the engineer who received their vocational training as an integrated part of their liberal arts education have something which the more specialized or professional school cannot give.

The fact that Colorado College, Dartmouth, Denison, Haverford, Lafayette, Swarthmore, and Union combine engineering with the liberal arts is a strong endorsement of the scheme. An encouraging development from the other side is the inclusion in the technical programs of the Case School, Drexel Institute, California Institute of Technology, Purdue, Rensselaer, Worcester, and the Massachusetts Institute of Technology of required courses in the humanities and social studies.

Curricula in the technical schools are becoming more liberal and those in many liberal arts colleges are including more vocational implementation. It should be pointed out, however, that much of the training for several vocations is really nothing more than a special organization of courses which are really liberal arts courses. For example, a sound curriculum in journalism might well be constructed from the following courses culled from the current offerings in a liberal arts college:

ENGLISH	Practical Writing, Writing for Effect, Introduction to Journalism, News Writing, Feature Writing, Short Story Writing, Creative Writing, Poetry, Fiction, Drama, Biography, American Literature, English Literature, European Literature, Literary Criticism, Chaucer, Shakespeare
ART	Appreciation of Art
ECONOMICS	Principles of Economics
SCIENCE	Survey of Natural Science
HISTORY	European History, American History, Far Eastern History

FOREIGN LANGUAGES	French or German or Spanish or Latin or Russian
MUSIC	Music Appreciation, History of Music
PHILOSOPHY	History of Philosophy
POLITICAL SCIENCE	American Government, International Relations, Law for the Citizen
PSYCHOLOGY	Principles of Psychology, Mental Hygiene, Social Psychology, Abnormal Psychology
RELIGION	Religions of the United States, Old Testament, New Testament
SOCIOLOGY	Principles of Sociology
SPEECH	Fundamentals of Speech, Interpretative Reading, Acting, Stage Directing, Persuasion, History of the Theater.

Similarly, curricula could be constructed for government service, household management, personnel management, social work, business administration, scientific research, and all pre-professional study.

Several four-year arts colleges have expanded their programs into a fifth year, and offer the master's degree in certain departments where they are exceptionally equipped. This is true of Beloit, Bucknell, Colorado College, Haverford, Kalamazoo, MacMurray, Middlebury, and Mills, among others. Middlebury has developed its work in languages to the point that it is offering the doctorate in that one field. The number of students in the graduate division of any of these colleges is ordinarily not large. To serve students who might otherwise be unable to attend graduate school, and to provide a fifth year for prospective high school teachers, this graduate instruction is perhaps justified; in most cases, however, the student would probably profit more from study in a fully developed graduate school of a university.

Every college should be encouraged to develop its own individuality and pattern of instruction. So variant are the locales, sizes, faculties, equipment, and support of colleges and universities that each institution must work out its own methods of rendering the highest service. There is no need for uniformity in higher education in America any more than there is in its churches, its businesses, its magazines, or its towns and cities. Notwithstanding the forces that have tended toward uniformity and standardization, there has been considerable diversity among American institutions of higher learning.

For example, the Catholic University of America frankly states that it hopes to make better churchmen of its students, and assures non-Catholics that they must live in such an atmosphere if they attend; several other denominational colleges are organized around similar responsibilities toward their church. St. John's College returns to the Greeks for the core of its curriculum in "the Great Books," Antioch has brought distinction upon itself by alternating study with work experience, Swarthmore by intensive scholarly concentration. Middlebury has specialized in the languages, Bennington in the arts, Scripps in the humanities. Berea, which serves a limited geographical area, has developed an unique program of service to a mountain people with marked characteristics; Dartmouth is seeking an "all-American" type through its policy of geographical distribution; Pomona, situated on the Pacific coast, places emphasis upon our relations with the Orient; Knox, in the heart of the Middle West, has emphasized the essentially American elements in our culture; Carleton, strengthened by the Frank B. Kellogg Foundation in International Relations, offers unusual opportunities for study in that field.

These are but examples of differences in college offerings and methods which enrich the opportunities of students and add to the interest and significance of the institutions themselves. Standardizing agencies, like the regional associations of colleges and secondary schools, should allow their members complete freedom in establishing their goals. It is a happy circumstance in America that such organizations, almost without exception, are voluntary agencies; when governmental agencies become involved in curricular standardization, freedom is likely to disappear.

But we must not allow our enthusiasm for institutional individuality, or for any pattern of instruction, or for any administrative device, to overbalance the needs of the student. The purpose of liberal education is not realized in the selection and arrangement of courses in accordance with any pattern or method but in the happiness and significance of the lives of those who are influenced by the programs adopted. The chief danger in curriculum planning is that it will eventually be made to serve the purpose of some educational theory or philosophical point of view or of some vested interest rather than the welfare of the student himself.

What colleges of liberal education need is not so much strict schemes of instruction or fixed methods of procedure as devotion to the ideal of freedom and effectiveness in guiding the individual freedom of each student in ways that will mean his highest development. Each college, therefore, should seek more aggressively to build and administer its curriculum to enable the student to develop a truly integrated personality. More individualized instruction and guidance, more flexibility in requirements, less domination by departments during the period of general education, and more encouragement to seminar and honors and tutorial work are steps in this direction.

CHAPTER VII

Extracurricular Education

As the increased leisure promised us by peace and material prosperity becomes more a reality, training for the use of this time in activities which enrich rather than impoverish personality becomes an expanding duty of the college. The enjoyment a mature person finds in reading great literature, listening to exquisite music, contemplating sculpture or painting or architectural masterpieces, witnessing drama or other spectacles, is not the result of casual circumstances; to a large extent it must be learned; good taste is not acquired through heredity, but is a product of environment plus training in the perception of distinctions. Enjoyment requires the proper atmosphere and a feeling that there is time to relax; four years in college provide the time and should provide the atmosphere.

A student is in the classroom only fifteen or sixteen hours a week, and even if he spends twenty to thirty hours more in assigned reading, solving problems, and writing reports he still has a large part of the week left at his disposal. It is in the use of this time that he may find his greatest opportunity for development, but it is the unusual student who does so. The failure on the part of so many students to make significant use of their leisure time is the basis for probably the most serious criticism that could be passed on the average college situation in the period between the two world wars. A reasonable amount of time should, of course, be devoted to avowed recreation—games, listening to the radio, conversation, "dates," movies, dancing, and daydreaming—but these should not be the only interests outside the classroom.

Equally injurious would be a program of working for room,

board, or cash which allowed no time for anything but classes and study; many a farseeing student has decided that, rather than spend all his free time in working to pay his college expenses, he would borrow part of the money and pay it back after graduation, when his ability to earn should be greater. For the student whose financial circumstances force him to work at remunerative employment, the problem is to secure work which will have educational or recreational value, such as departmental or library assistantships and paid managerships of student activities.

In the use of his leisure time a student in an American college is not left to his own devices. He is surrounded with a multitude of opportunities for activities on a voluntary basis. So extensive and time-consuming are these nonclassroom allurements that many critics of the colleges feel they are in open competition with scholarship and tend to defeat the fundamental purpose for which the institution exists. The problem that finally faces the student of broad interests becomes one of choosing among dozens of possible ways to spend leisure time. Most students probably need as much guidance from faculty advisers in planning their out-of-class activities as in selecting courses of study best adapted to their needs.

For many students, recreational sports and intercollegiate athletics are the chief extracurricular attraction. We have already expressed the conviction that the cure for abuses in this area is wider participation; here the college with limited enrollment has a real advantage, for every student can be on a team. The same principle holds true for all other activities; the college should try to provide enough variety so that each individual can find the particular niche where he is both happy and effective.

The college theater is not only a laboratory for the speech student; it is a recreational-educational activity for any student who likes to act or to construct scenery. The choir, glee club, orchestra, and band are not professional in purpose, though their work may be of the highest quality, as in the St. Olaf Choir, the Harvard Glee Club, and the University of Illinois Field Band. They are intended for the amateur who wants to sing or play acceptably. Some colleges are offering free instruction in "recreational piano" lessons with no thought of credit or professional ambitions. For many students, perhaps the surest path to mature music appreciation runs via playing a trombone or the piano for fun.

More successful lawyers, preachers, and statesmen have probably received their training in speaking through extracurricular activities than in the classroom. Debates, oratorical contests, radio broadcasts, and forum discussions, plus the parliamentary procedure of the literary society or departmental club, have provided the competition and stimulus needed to develop leadership. In like manner, writing for the college paper or humorous magazine has trained thousands of successful journalists, and improved the written style of many more who never worked for a city newspaper. Democratically conducted student government can be highly educative, especially if real responsibilities are shared by the administration with the students. Church activities should be a natural part of the life of the average student; properly directed, by local ministers or a college chaplain or the Y.M.C.A.-Y.W.C.A., they develop a sense of social responsibility as effectively as courses in ethics and in many cases result in lifelong practical interest in religious and social agencies.

Colleges without fraternities and sororities are persuaded that this arrangement is more democratic, for there are no caste lines drawn; more beneficial to campus morale, for loyalties are to the college as a whole rather than to a smaller group; and more economical, for there are no national dues, no chapter fees, no fraternity jewelry, and no privately owned houses which are a constant financial drain. Such colleges can plan their dormitory system as a social as well as a residential scheme, can exercise closer faculty and administrative supervision over the living, study, and health conditions of all students, and can avoid the frequent heartaches and hysteria of rushing and pledging plus the dangers of initiations. Some colleges are persuaded that, by eliminating "rush week" and "hell week," they have added two good weeks of study and effective classroom work to the college year.

On the other hand, colleges with the fraternity-sorority tradition are convinced that, properly integrated with the total college program, these organizations can do good work in social education. A good fraternity can help its pledges through the complexities of the early days of college, it can provide help and supervision in the establishment of effective study habits, it can awaken new interests and cut across departmental lines in the nightly "bull sessions," and it can teach manners and etiquette effectively because of the esprit of the group.

To accomplish these purposes, there should be sufficient chapters on a campus to permit all who desire fraternity life to receive its benefits. The extra expense of fraternity membership, therefore, should be kept at a minimum; elaborate, overbuilt, costly houses should be forbidden by college and national headquarters alike. On some campuses, to secure the benefit of the dormitory as well as the fraternity social scheme, the colleges require that students live in the dormitory during their freshmen year, moving into the fraternity house only after they have learned to live together as freshmen. Probably the right answer to the fraternity "problem" is to have colleges of both types: those with fraternities should work to make them a coordinated and effective part of the whole college plan; those without fraternities should give special attention to all-college social programs supplemented by social activities carried on by smaller groups in ways that will provide opportunities for all students to become socially mature.

Every campus should have series of lectures, concerts, and other events of high educational value in addition to its formal courses. These should be selected and scheduled, not for the benefit of the faculty or the townspeople, but primarily for students, and their attendance should be encouraged and for some events required.

Summer vacations present great opportunities which are seldom fully used. The student without funds will probably seek full-time employment to help finance the next year of college; the veteran and the older man may wish to hasten the date of graduation and decide to attend the summer session. But the average student rejoices at the prospect of freedom from the classroom, and pushes all idea of his college program out of his mind from June until September. For the student who has concentrated heavily on studies during the year, this may be a wise policy; but for the vast majority, the summer should provide a laboratory period in which many of the ideas argued over in the classroom can be given practical trial. For the student of social science, perhaps an assistantship in a summer camp or a settlement house, a hospital or a government agency, would provide material for the next year's class discussions. For the scientist, practical engineering or field trips or work as a guide in a national park will be putting theories to work. For the student of art, music, or literature, the long uninterrupted weeks of summer give the leisure to accomplish those big time-consuming projects—the portrait or statue, the sonata learned or the composition completed, the essay written or the book list read. Yale College, in its new educational program, is requiring that all students outline a project of reading or research before leaving for the summer, and return in the fall ready to stand examination over the books assigned or the project completed.

Every student in the long run must be responsible for his own progress and the earlier he recognizes this the better, for he is then more likely to cultivate the habits necessary to achieve maturity. Nowhere is this comment more relevant than in respect to the use of books. No instructor will admit that a student can learn without a teacher what could be learned with his help. Even if the instructor does nothing but criticize the student's performance, he saves hours of time and wasted effort. This is particularly true in the tool subjects and the arts; piano or drawing or mathematics or French without a teacher may sound very attractive at first, but nine out of ten who begin such an undertaking will soon fall by the way. The cross-fertilization of minds in the classroom, the adding of the oral interpretation of the text to the reading of it, the emphasis of selection by the professor, all help to increase the student's understanding. But these external aids are short-lived. College days are soon over and the graduate faces the necessity of finding his motivation and inspiration within himself.

It is necessary, therefore, for the student, while he is in college, to acquire the habit of leisure reading for cultural values, for a few hours each week, and for longer stretches in the summer. What are the "great books" which should be part of the cultural reading background of an educated person? Dr. Eliot filled fifty volumes with his selections; Sir John Lubbock picked a hundred titles; Theodore Roosevelt chose a library to take with him on his African trip; John Erskine prepared a list for the Army during World War I. The latest list to arouse discussion is the St. John's College "Hundred Best Books," used as the basis for its curriculum. The principle involved here, of avoiding the textbook and seeking primary sources, is an excellent one, but it seems uneconomical in time in the study of mathematics, languages, and the sciences; also, this list seems heavily overloaded in certain fields, light in others.

In the following list of books recommended for cultural reading, there is no implication that all are "musts." From three hundred and more titles, the "one hundred best" for one student should be quite different from the list for another. There should be books for every age level in college, from the sixteen-year-old adolescent to the mature man or woman. Many of these books are suitable for classroom use, and may be part of the reading prescribed in the student's courses. Some are to be skimmed through rapidly, others "chewed and digested," as Sir Francis Bacon advised. The careful reading of representative volumes from this list, which is arranged chronologically within each area, would mark a long step in the direction of general and liberal education for anyone who has learned how to read with understanding.

Cultural Reading in Literature and Philosophy

Each work of literature and philosophy is a reflection not only of the individual mind that created it but also of the society and thought of the age in which it was written. For a period of time, therefore, we are privileged to live in another age and see life through the mind of another person. We meet hundreds of individual characters, some from history and others created in the mind and experience of the author. We enter into their thoughts and emotions in a manner that is not permitted to us in our ordinary daily life.

The comedy of Rabelais and Cervantes and Fielding and Voltaire will make us laugh at mankind and at ourselves, so that our sense of balance is restored, whereas the tragedies of Sophocles or Dante, Shakespeare or Hawthorne or Tolstoi will, as Aristotle pointed out, purge our souls from the baser emotions and give them a feeling of uplift. In poetry we find a condensation of human experience, emotions, and ideas in a rhythmic word pattern which gives aesthetic pleasure to the ear and eye at the same time that it stimulates the mind. In the drama we can visualize the characters upon the stage or enter into the personalities of half a dozen different people through their own speech throughout the play. In the novel the reader has time for thorough analysis of inner motives and explanations of events, and for witnessing the complete development of characters. Unconsciously we find ourselves forming a philosophy of life from the many philosophies that are described to us by the characters and the authors we read. Such reading adds to the significance of living, gives it direction and purpose and makes the individual more fully aware of the meaning and possibilities of his own existence.

THE BIBLE—*Old Testament* (*c.* 2000 B.C. ff.)

HOMER—*Iliad; Odyssey* (*c.* 850 B.C.)

CONFUCIUS—*Analects of Spring and Autumn* (*c.* 500 B.C.)

AESCHYLUS—*Plays* (472–458 B.C.)

SOPHOCLES—*Plays* (451–401 B.C.)

EURIPIDES—*Plays* (438–407 B.C.)

PLATO—*Republic; Apology, Crito,* and *Phaedo* (4th Cent. B.C.)

ARISTOTLE—*Poetics, Rhetoric,* and *Ethics* (4th Cent. B.C.)

KALIDASA—*Shakuntala* (begun 1st Cent. B.C.)

VIRGIL—*Aeneid* (29–19 B.C.)

PLUTARCH—*Lives of Alexander and Caesar* (1st & 2nd Cent. A.D.)

THE BIBLE—*New Testament* (written A.D. 1st Cent., collected 4th Cent.)

MARCUS AURELIUS—*Meditations* (*c.* A.D. 178)

MOHAMMED—*The Koran* (*c.* A.D. 650)

Beowulf (*c.* 800)

DANTE—*The Divine Comedy* (1302)

BOCCACCIO—*The Decameron* (1353)

GEOFFREY CHAUCER—*Canterbury Tales* (1387–1400)

The Arabian Nights (collected *c.* 1500 [Burton's translation best])

RABELAIS—*Gargantua* (1535)

WILLIAM SHAKESPEARE—*Hamlet; King Lear; Othello; The Tempest; Twelfth Night* (1603–1611)

CERVANTES—*Don Quixote* (1605–1615)

MOLIÈRE—*Tartuffe* (1664)

JOHN MILTON—*Paradise Lost* (1667); *Areopagitica* (1644)

JOHN BUNYAN—*Pilgrim's Progress* (1678)

DANIEL DEFOE—*Robinson Crusoe* (1719); *Captain Singleton* (1720)

JONATHAN SWIFT—*Gulliver's Travels* (1726)

HENRY FIELDING—*Tom Jones* (1749)

VOLTAIRE—*Candide* (1752)

BENJAMIN FRANKLIN—*Autobiography* (1771–1790)

JAMES BOSWELL—*Life of Samuel Johnson* (1791)

JOHANN W. VON GOETHE—*Faust* (1808–1832)

JANE AUSTEN—*Pride and Prejudice* (1813)

JOHN KEATS—*Poems* (1817–1820)

WALTER SCOTT—*The Heart of Midlothian* (1818)

CHARLES LAMB—*Essays of Elia* (1823–1833)

ALFRED TENNYSON—*Poems* (1827–1892)

HONORÉ BALZAC—*Eugénie Grandet* (1833); *Père Goriot* (1834)

ROBERT BROWNING—*Poems* (1833–1889)

CHARLES DICKENS—*Pickwick Papers* (1827); *David Copperfield* (1850); *Great Expectations* (1861)

RALPH W. EMERSON—*Essays* (1841–1844)

THOMAS CARLYLE—*Past and Present* (1843)

ALEXANDRE DUMAS—*The Three Musketeers* (1844)

HENRY D. THOREAU—*Walden* (1845)

EDGAR ALLAN POE—*Tales* (1845)

CHARLOTTE BRONTË—*Jane Eyre* (1847)

WILLIAM M. THACKERAY—*Vanity Fair* (1848)

NATHANIEL HAWTHORNE—*The Scarlet Letter* (1850)

GEORGE BORROW—*Lavengro* (1851)

CHARLES KINGSLEY—*Hypatia* (1851)

HERMAN MELVILLE—*Moby Dick* (1851)

WALT WHITMAN—*Leaves of Grass* (1855)

GUSTAVE FLAUBERT—*Madame Bovary* (1856)

CHARLES READE—*The Cloister and the Hearth* (1861)

VICTOR HUGO—*Les Misérables* (1862)

ERNEST RENAN—*The Life of Jesus* (1863)

GEORGE ELIOT—*Romola* (1863)

LEO TOLSTOI—*War and Peace* (1865–1872)

LEWIS CARROLL—*Alice in Wonderland* (1865)

FEODOR DOSTOEVSKY—*Crime and Punishment* (1866)

HENRY JAMES—*Short Stories* (1875–1916)

HENRIK IBSEN—*A Doll's House* (1879); *Ghosts* (1881); *An Enemy of the People* (1882)

SAMUEL CLEMENS—*Life on the Mississippi* (1883); *Huckleberry Finn* (1884)

THOMAS HARDY—*The Mayor of Casterbridge* (1886); *The Dynasts* (1904–1908)

RUDYARD KIPLING—*Short Stories* (1888–1926); *Kim* (1901)

ARTHUR CONAN DOYLE—*The Adventures of Sherlock Holmes* (1891)

WILLIAM BUTLER YEATS—*Poems* (1895–1940)

GERHARDT HAUPTMANN—*The Sunken Bell* (1896)

G. LOWES DICKINSON—*The Greek View of Life* (1896); *A Modern Symposium* (1905)

WILLIAM JAMES—*Papers in Philosophy* (1897–1909)

EDMOND ROSTAND—*Cyrano de Bergerac* (1898)

JOSEPH CONRAD—*Lord Jim* (1900); *Nostromo* (1904); *Victory* (1915)

THOMAS MANN—*Buddenbrooks* (1900); *The Magic Mountain* (1924); the *Joseph* series (1933–1938)

SAMUEL BUTLER—*The Way of all Flesh* (1903)

GEORGE BERNARD SHAW—*Man and Superman* (1903); *Major Barbara* (1907)

WILLIAM H. HUDSON—*Green Mansions* (1904)

ANATOLE FRANCE—*Penguin Island* (1908)

EDITH WHARTON—*Ethan Frome* (1911)

SOMERSET MAUGHAM—*Of Human Bondage* (1916)

KNUT HAMSUN—*Growth of the Soil* (1917)

WILLA CATHER—*My Ántonia* (1918)

LOUIS UNTERMEYER—*Modern British and American Poetry* (1920 ff.)

SIGRID UNDSET—*Kristin Lavransdatter* (1920–1922)

SINCLAIR LEWIS—*Babbitt* (1922); *Arrowsmith* (1925)

JOHN GALSWORTHY—*The Forsyte Saga* (1922)

OLE E. RÖLVAAG—*Giants in the Earth* (1924)

EMILY DICKINSON—*Complete Poems* (1924)

JAMES JOYCE—*Ulysses* (1925)

ROMAIN ROLLAND—*Jean Christophe* (1925–1927)

EVERETT DEAN MARTIN—*The Meaning of a Liberal Education* (1926)

STEPHEN VINCENT BENÉT—*John Brown's Body* (1928)

H. H. RICHARDSON—*Ultima Thule* (1929)

EUGENE O'NEILL—*Mourning Becomes Electra* (1931)

MORRIS COHEN—*Reason and Nature* (1931)

PEARL BUCK—*The Good Earth* (1931)

FRANZ WERFEL—*Forty Days of Musa Dagh* (1933)

JAMES FARRELL—*Studs Lonigan* (1935)

IRWIN EDMAN—*Four Ways of Philosophy* (1937)

JOHN DOS PASSOS—*U.S.A.* (1938)

BALLOU, SPIEGELBERG, and FRIESS—*The Bible of the World* (1939)

SHOLEM ASCH—*The Nazarene* (1939)

SIDNEY HOOK—*John Dewey* (1939)

JOHN STEINBECK—*The Grapes of Wrath* (1939)

MAGAZINES—*Saturday Review of Literature, Atlantic Monthly, Harper's, Kenyon Review*

Cultural Reading in the Fine Arts

The best way to know and appreciate the fine arts is to have direct personal contact with them as a creating participant or a concert and gallery attendant, but reading about artists or musicians and their work and the influences of their times can be a valuable supplement to these direct experiences, and for some people must take the place of the experience itself. Those who cannot visit the art galleries can at least peruse the excellent volumes of reproductions, and although the best introduction to music may be an album of symphony or opera records, a book in hand may well heighten the appreciation.

BENVENUTO CELLINI—*Autobiography* (16th Cent.)

VASARI—*Lives of the Most Celebrated Artists* (16th Cent.)

THOMAS BULFINCH—*The Age of Fable* (1855)

WALTER PATER—*The Renaissance* (1873)

JOHN A. SYMONDS—*The Renaissance in Italy* (1875–1887)

SIR CHARLES PARRY—*Evolution of the Art of Music* (1893)

DMITRI MEREZHKOWSKY—*The Romance of Leonardo da Vinci* (1902)

HENRY ADAMS—*Mont-Saint-Michel and Chartres* (1904)

ROMAIN ROLLAND—*Michelangelo* (1905); *Beethoven* (1903)

MONTROSE MOSES—*Famous Actor Families in America* (1906)

JOSEPH MCSPADDEN—*Famous Painters of America* (1907)

G. F. YOUNG—*The Medici* (1909)

JAMES G. HUNEKER—*Steeplejack* (1920)

JOSEPH PENNELL—*The Graphic Arts* (1921)

MARION BAUER and ETHEL PEYSER —*How Music Grew* (1925)

LEWIS MUMFORD—*Sticks and Stones* (1924); *The Brown Decades* (1931)

HELEN GARDNER—*Art Through the Ages* (1926); *Understanding the Arts* (1932)

CARL SANDBURG—*The American Songbag* (1927)

R. H. WILENSKY—*The Modern Movement in Art* (1927)

GEORGE ARLISS—*Up the Years from Bloomsbury* (1927)

OSCAR HAGEN—*Art Epochs and Their Leaders* (1927)

CLARENCE J. BULLIET—*Apples and Madonnas* (1927)

HELEN PARKHURST—*Beauty* (1930)

THOMAS CRAVEN—*Men of Art* (1931); *Modern Art* (1934)

JOHN TASKER HOWARD—*Our American Music* (1931)

FRANK LLOYD WRIGHT—*Autobiography* (1932)

MARCIA DAVENPORT—*Mozart* (1932)

GEORGE JEAN NATHAN—*Intimate Notebooks* (1932)

JOSEPH WOOD KRUTCH—*Experience and Art* (1932)

DIEGO RIVERA—*Portrait of America* (1934)

CAHILL and BARR—*Art in America* (1935)

HENDRIK VAN LOON—*The Arts* (1937)

THOMAS HART BENTON—*An Artist in America* (1937)

DEEMS TAYLOR—*Of Men and Music* (1937)

W. J. TURNER—*Mozart, The Man and His Works* (1938)

AARON COPLAND—*What to Listen for in Music* (1939)

F. RAMSEY and C. E. SMITH—*Jazzmen* (1939)

GEORGE SLOCOMBE—*Rebels of Art* (1939)

PEYTON BOSWELL—*Modern American Painting* (1939)

T. HAMLIN—*Architecture Through the Ages* (1940)

DAVID EWEN—*Pioneers in Music* (1940)

MAGAZINES—*Etude, Theatre Arts Monthly, Architectural Forum, Modern Music*

Cultural Reading in the Social Studies

History is primarily a written record, and most of the great contributions of economists, sociologists, and political scientists have been expressed in their own written word. What better way of understanding our own problems than to see those same problems worked upon by the Greeks in Thucydides, by the Romans in Gibbon, or by Americans interpreted by Adams or Beard? The nature of government is analyzed by Alexander Hamilton, Edmund Burke, James Bryce, and Stuart Chase, but it is illuminated even more vividly in the biographies of outstanding governmental leaders such as Napoleon, Disraeli, Abraham Lincoln, and Queen Victoria; and the reading of Lincoln Steffens's autobiography is more revealing than the perusal of any textbook.

THUCYDIDES—*History* (5th Cent. B.C.)

HERODOTUS—*History* (5th Cent. B.C.)

ST. AUGUSTINE—*The City of God* (A.D. 413–426)

MACHIAVELLI—*The Prince* (1513)

SIR THOMAS MORE—*Utopia* (1516)

BLAISE PASCAL—*Pensées* (1662)

SAMUEL PEPYS—*Diary* (1669)

JEAN J. ROUSSEAU—*The Social Contract* (1762)

ADAM SMITH—*The Wealth of Nations* (1776)

EDWARD GIBBON—*History of the Decline and Fall of the Roman Empire* (1776)

ALEXANDER HAMILTON et al.—*The Federalist Papers* (1787)

EDMUND BURKE—*Reflections on the Revolution in France* (1790)

THOMAS PAINE—*The Rights of Man* (1792)

CLAUSEWITZ—*On War* (1832)

WILLIAM PRESCOTT—*History of the Conquest of Mexico* (1843)

JOHN STUART MILL—*Principles of Political Economy* (1848); *Liberty* (1859); *Representative Government* (1861); *Utilitarianism* (1863)

KARL MARX—*The Communist Manifesto* (1848); *Capital* (1867–1894)

FRANCIS PARKMAN—*The Conspiracy of Pontiac* (1851)

HENRY MAINE—*Ancient Law* (1861)

WALTER BAGEHOT—*Physics and Politics* (1869)

SAMUEL BUTLER—*Erewhon* (1872)

JOHN R. GREEN—*A Short History of the English People* (1874)

JAMES BRYCE—*The American Commonwealth* (1888)

EDWARD BELLAMY—*Looking Backward* (1888)

ALFRED T. MAHAN—*Influence of Sea Power upon History* (1890)

WILLIAM JAMES—*Principles of Psychology* (1890)

THORSTEIN VEBLEN—*The Theory of the Leisure Class* (1899)

J. B. BURY—*A History of Greece* (1900); *The Idea of Progress* (1920)

BOOKER T. WASHINGTON—*Up From Slavery* (1901)

JANE ADDAMS—*Twenty Years at Hull House* (1910)

HENRY O. TAYLOR—*The Mediaeval Mind* (1911)

GAMALIEL BRADFORD—*Lee the American* (1912)

NIKOLAI LENIN—*The State and Revolution* (1918)

OSWALD SPENGLER—*The Decline of the West* (1918–1923)

J. M. KEYNES—*The Economic Consequences of the Peace* (1919)

H. G. WELLS—*An Outline of History* (1920)

HENDRIK VAN LOON—*Ancient Man* (1920)

WILLIAM E. DODD—*Woodrow Wilson and His Work* (1920)

EDWARD BOK—*The Americanization of Edward Bok* (1920)

J. H. ROBINSON—*The Mind in the Making* (1921)

LYTTON STRACHEY—*Queen Victoria* (1921)

GRAHAM WALLAS—*Our Social Heritage* (1921)

OTTO JESPERSEN—*Language, Its Nature, Development, and Origin* (1922)

LEWIS MUMFORD—*The Story of Utopias* (1922); *The Culture of Cities* (1938)

CLAUDE BOWERS—*Jefferson and Hamilton* (1925)

ADOLF HITLER—*My Battle* (1925)

RICHARD TAWNEY—*Religion and the Rise of Capitalism* (1926)

SIR NORMAN ANGELL—*The Public Mind* (1926)

CARL SANDBURG—*Abraham Lincoln* (1926–1939)

LEWIS BROWNE—*This Believing World* (1926)

J. H. RANDALL—*The Making of the Modern Mind* (1926)

T. E. LAWRENCE—*Seven Pillars of Wisdom* (1926)

V. L. PARRINGTON—*Main Currents in American Thought* (1927–1930)

EMIL LUDWIG—*Napoleon* (1927)

ANDRÉ MAUROIS—*Disraeli* (1927)

HAROLD LAMB—*Genghis Khan* (1927)

R. S. LYND—*Middletown* (1929); *Middletown in Transition* (1937)

FRANCIS HACKETT—*Henry VIII* (1929)

STUART CHASE—*Men and Machines* (1929); *Goals for America* (1942)

JAMES T. ADAMS—*The Epic of America* (1931)

LINCOLN STEFFENS—*Autobiography* (1931)

HENRY F. PRINGLE—*Theodore Roosevelt* (1931)

A. A. BERLE and G. C. MEANS—*The Modern Corporation and Private Property* (1932)

EDNA HEIDBREDER—*Seven Psychologies* (1933)

MARQUIS JAMES—*Andrew Jackson* (1933–1937)

RUTH BENEDICT—*Patterns of Culture* (1934)

LOUIS ADAMIC—*The Native's Return* (1934); *A Nation of Nations* (1945)

WILL DURANT—*Our Oriental Heritage* (1935)

VINCENT SHEEAN—*Personal History* (1935)

T. V. SMITH—*The Promise of American Politics* (1936)

THURMAN ARNOLD—*The Folklore of Capitalism* (1937)

KARL MENNINGER—*The Human Mind* (1937)

HERBERT HARRIS—*American Labor* (1938)

SIGMUND FREUD—*The Basic Writings* (1938)

GEORGE COULTON—*Mediaeval Panorama* (1938)

JOHN DEWEY—*Intelligence in the Modern World* (1939)

HAROLD NICOLSON—*Diplomacy* (1939)

KAREN HORNEY—*New Ways of Psychoanalysis* (1939)

R. G. COLLINGWOOD—*The New Leviathan* (1942)

MERLE CURTI—*The Growth of American Thought* (1943)

W. C. LANGER—*Psychology and Human Living* (1943)

CHARLES and MARY BEARD—*Basic History of the United States* (1944)

GUNNAR MYRDAL—*An American Dilemma* (1944)

D. W. BROGAN—*The American Character* (1944)

JACQUES BARZUN—*Teacher in America* (1945)

MAGAZINES—*Yale Review, Foreign Affairs, Time, Newsweek, Fortune*

Cultural Reading in Science

It is often assumed that science can be taught only in the laboratory, and therefore it is quite refreshing to have a great contemporary chemist, President Conant of Harvard, tell us that too little emphasis has been placed upon the history of science and the way in which scientific ideas have grown in the minds of men. It is true that many scientists have been poor writers, but others have put the very essence of their work into the written word, as in the writings of Darwin, Osborne, or Cannon. In other cases, the work of scientists has been interpreted by men of letters who vivified the experiences of the laboratories, the struggles of the experimenter, and the final success. For many readers the understanding that comes from reading the life of Pasteur or Osler or Madame Curie may give almost as much insight into the methods of science as many hours spent in the laboratory.

ARISTOTLE—*Natural Philosophy* (*c.* 350 B.C.)

LEONARDO DA VINCI—*Notebooks* (*c.* 1500)

FRANCIS BACON—*Instauratio Magna* (1605–1620)

SIR CHARLES LYELL—*Principles of Geology* (1830)

CHARLES DARWIN—*The Origin of Species* (1859)

HERBERT SPENCER—*First Principles* (1862)

THOMAS HUXLEY—*Lay Sermons* (1870); *Collected Essays* (1893)

OLIVER LODGE—*Pioneers of Science* (1892)

RENÉ VALÉRY-RADOT—*The Life of Pasteur* (1900)

MAURICE MAETERLINCK—*Life of the Bee* (1902)

SIR WILLIAM OSLER—*Collected Essays* (1904–1908)

ALFRED N. WHITEHEAD—*Introduction to Mathematics* (1910)

HENRI POINCARÉ—*Foundations of Science* (1913)

FIELDING H. GARRISON—*Introduction to the History of Medicine* (1913)

HENRY F. OSBORN—*Men of the Old Stone Age* (1915)

RICHARD GREGORY—*Discovery* (1916)

WILLIAM BEEBE—*Jungle Peace* (1918)

E. E. SLOSSON—*Creative Chemistry* (1919)

ALBERT EINSTEIN—*Relativity: the Special and the General Theory* (1920)

J. B. S. HALDANE—*Daedalus* (1924)

HARVEY W. CUSHING—*Life of Sir William Osler* (1925)

WILLIAM BRAGG—*Concerning the Nature of Things* (1925)

PAUL DE KRUIF—*Microbe Hunters* (1926)

HARRY A. OVERSTREET—*About Ourselves* (1927)

ROBERT and ADA YERKES—*The Great Apes* (1929)

H. G. WELLS and J. HUXLEY—*The Science of Life* (1929)

M. HOLLAND and H. PRINGLE—*Industrial Explorers* (1929)

HOWARD W. HAGGARD—*Devils, Drugs, and Doctors* (1929); *Alcohol Explored* (1942)

JAMES JEANS—*The Mysterious Universe* (1930)

BERNARD JAFFE—*Crucibles* (1930); *Outposts of Science* (1935); *Men of Science in America* (1944)

E. T. BELL—*Queen of the Sciences* (1931)

ERIC HOLMYARD—*Makers of Chemistry* (1931)

DAVID DIETZ—*The Story of Science* (1931)

ALDOUS HUXLEY—*Brave New World* (1932)

FREDERICK PRESCOTT—*Modern Chemistry* (1932)

HENDRIK VAN LOON—*Geography* (1932)

W. B. CANNON—*Wisdom of the Body* (1932)

ROY HOSKINS—*Tides of Life* (1933)

HARVEY LEMON—*From Galileo to Cosmic Rays* (1934)

J. LEONARD—*Tools of Tomorrow* (1935)

HANS ZINSSER—*Rats, Lice, and History* (1935)

DONALD C. PEATTIE—*An Almanac for Moderns* (1935); *Green Laurels* (1936); *A Prairie Grove* (1938)

PAUL B. SEARS—*Deserts on the March* (1935)

CRONEIS and KRUMBEIN—*Down to Earth* (1936)

LANCELOT HOGBEN—*Mathematics for the Million* (1936); *Science for the Citizen* (1938)

K. DARROW—*The Renaissance of Physics* (1936)

VICTOR HEISER—*An American Doctor's Odyssey* (1936)

HENRY WILLIAMSON—*Salar the Salmon* (1936)

MALVINA HOFFMAN—*Heads and Tales* (1936)

ALEX FINDLAY—*A Hundred Years of Chemistry* (1937)

ALAN F. GUTTMACHER—*Into This Universe* (1937)

RICHARD GOLDSCHMIDT—*Ascaris: The Biologist's Story of Life* (1937)

EVE CURIE—*Madame Curie* (1937)

E. A. HOOTON—*Apes, Men, and Morons* (1937)

WARDER C. ALLEE—*Social Life of Animals* (1938)

C. L. FENTON—*Our Amazing Earth* (1938); *Our Living World* (1943)

JOHN H. BRADLEY—*Patterns of Survival* (1938)

ERNEST R. TRATTNER—*Architects of Ideas* (1938)

J. D. BERNAL—*The Social Function of Science* (1939)

H. LEVY—*Modern Science* (1939)

CONRAD MATSCHOSS—*Great Engineers* (1939)

AMRAM SCHEINFELDT—*You and Heredity* (1939)

GEORGE R. STEWART—*Storm* (1941); *Names on the Land* (1945); *Man: An Autobiography* (1946)

HARLOW SHAPLEY—*A Treasury of Science* (1943)

FRITZ KAHN—*Man in Structure and Function* (1943)

H. W. RICKETT—*The Green Earth* (1943)

SIDNEY A. FOX—*Your Eyes* (1944)

FOREST R. MOULTON—*Autobiography of Science* (1945)

MAGAZINES—*Science News Letter, Scientific Monthly, Nature*

It is not too much to expect of an educated person that he own a reasonable number of books as a personal library. Borrowed books lack the individuality he should seek; our own books may be personalized by associations, by notations in the margins, by the desire to keep them handy for rereading or reference. When graduates set up homes, they will want libraries; why not start building them in college? The purchase of a few dozen books each year will tend to establish the habit of cultural reading.

But it is also reasonable to expect that most of the reading material used by students will be supplied by the college library. A liberal arts college library differs notably from a university library. In the college there is no need for an exhaustive covering of research and professional fields, and therefore the collection can be limited in size. A reasonable working collection might contain two hundred books per student, and after this point is reached, old and outmoded books should be discarded as rapidly as new ones are added. The card catalogue should be made as useful as possible for the undergraduate, with many cross references; but he should be encouraged to go into the stacks and see the books on the shelves—of course, this mean "open shelves." A librarian who understands classroom requirements and the significance of leisure properly employed, and who loves students at the same time that he loves books, is an indispensable member of every college staff. Browsing rooms, dormitory libraries, and liberal borrowing privileges will promote cultural reading; words of encouragement from a member of the faculty may start a student on a lifetime habit in the use of books. There is no way open to a student by which he can so surely gain for himself the objectives of general and liberal education as through persistent and discriminating reading.

CHAPTER VIII

Teachers and Administrators

The chief function of a college is teaching, and the teacher and the student are obviously the two most important persons in the organization. It was undoubtedly the memory of this fact that led President Garfield to describe the best college as a log with Mark Hopkins on one end and the student on the other. Mark Hopkins was a great teacher; may his tribe increase. Any institution which can attract and hold together even a small body of good teachers is a good college, regardless of any other circumstance. The opportunity that a college gives to each of its students to come into individual relations with unusually significant personalities and to have the benefit of their instruction and inspiration is the most precious gift these institutions have to offer. This relationship between teacher and student represents the fundamental purpose of a true college; all other features of its program, including administration and finance, should be subservient to this end. Even scholarly research must not be unduly emphasized for its own sake. It is probably true that no one can carry on the highest type of teaching and be indifferent to the search after new truth. However, there is a great difference between an interest in research for the sake of teaching and a neglect of teaching for the sake of research. The interest of a college teacher centers in the student and not in the progress of knowledge as such, important as that may be. Upon this distinction rests the difference between a true college and a true university.

It is not an easy task to find the teachers a college needs. The graduate schools, where the majority of college teachers are trained, are not organized primarily to develop good teachers.

Their chief emphasis for the past seventy years has been upon training scholars and research workers in ever narrower fields. Teaching at the college level would probably be greatly improved if the graduate schools of the country would give greater consideration to the needs of prospective college teachers. There has been considerable discussion of this matter in college and university circles during recent years, but as yet little seems to have been accomplished. The graduate school faculty, themselves trained in research, naturally look upon research interests as the only legitimate basis for the doctor's degree, and frown upon any other basis as obviously inferior.

However, unless we are prepared to admit that teaching itself as a vocation is inferior to a career in research, there is no reason to assume that a program of studies carefully designed for the training of teachers is less worthy of recognition than one organized to develop skills in the techniques and methods of research. Such a course of study should not be easier or less exacting than the research and thesis course, but it should be different, broader in the fields of knowledge required, more directly tied to the needs of the college classroom. The graduate schools may need to add to their faculties some new members whose own interests are in this direction rather than the other.

College teachers who fulfill the ideal we have suggested have actually existed in the flesh—a Bliss Perry or a William Lyon Phelps, men who have attained international fame as teachers and who have described the work of a true teacher fully and sympathetically in their autobiographies. Every college probably has at least one outstanding teacher, the persistent topic of conversation among the undergraduates and the alumni, beloved of many, and a continuing influence in their lives long after graduation. Those colleges with two or more are indeed fortunate. In selecting new members of the faculty, the college president or dean or committee should be concerned primarily as to whether the candidate gives promise of developing into such a center of influence. Nor is this merely a matter of the length of time a faculty member remains, though obviously the longer he stays the stronger the bonds of influence and student loyalty are likely to become. However, we have all seen young college teachers leap almost immediately into such a position of power, and we have seen men after thirty years on the same faculty dried up into almost complete nonentity.

Assuming that such a faculty can be found, what is the function of the administration of a college?—essentially, to free the teachers to perform their true function, and to encourage them in that performance. The work of a president, deans, and other administrative officers must in the long run be judged in terms of its helpfulness to teachers. However, a college has become more than a teacher, a log, and a student; the log has grown into a campus and plant which require maintenance, repair, and expansion; finance looms large, both the securing of funds and their investment, and the collection and disbursement of student payments for tuition, room, board, and activities; personnel, even when it is organized upon democratic principles, requires an executive branch and a court of appeal for the arbitration of disputes.

The administration is formed to render these services, and they are necessary—but they are by no means the central function of the college; that can be performed only by the teacher. It is because of this fact that administrators in liberal arts colleges frequently ask for faculty rank and teach a course or two— they want to feel that they are participating in the real work of college education. Good administrators will try to remain teachers in spirit, so that they can understand the problems of the classroom, feel the pulse of the student body through more than occasional contact, and keep their minds alive to the content of the curriculum.

But to what extent should teachers be asked to perform administrative tasks? On some campuses the number of faculty committees involved in what are essentially administrative responsibilities is so great that it is almost impossible for the conscientious committee member to find time for proper preparation for his teaching, counseling with students, preparing and evaluating tests and assignments, building up the library and other equipment needed by his department, and following the research going on in his field—which are the important things he should be doing when not actually in the classroom.

There are skeptics, such as a former governor of Oklahoma, who insist that college teachers should spend their forty hours a week in actual classroom teaching if they are to be called workers. A typical college English teacher once made an inventory of his working week. It is true that he spent only fourteen hours in actual lectures and instruction in the classroom, which seems such an easy burden. But, since two of his five classes were in composition and he believed strongly in personal conferences on written work, his six hours of scheduled office hours usually proved insufficient, and had to be expanded to twelve. Fifty original papers averaging five hundred words each were being submitted by his students in writing for criticism each week, and try as he might he couldn't speed up the reading of these compositions, the evaluating of them, and the writing of useful comments upon them, to less than ten minutes per paper—a total of eight more hours.

By staggering the examinations given in his other three courses, he could have one set of twenty examination papers to grade each week—another four hours. His courses were in five different subjects; though he had heard of the professor who went into the classroom unprepared, using the same set of notes for thirty years and relying upon his position to bluff his way through the hour, this teacher was conscientious, and couldn't discuss the reading assigned to the students without doing it himself, at least in rapid review—result, another fourteen hours. The total has now reached fifty-two hours a week, and no time whatever has been allowed for reading up on recent research in the field of English literature, indulging in a little of that research himself, reading the new books so that he may make recommendations for additions to the college library, and perhaps writing a book himself. There is not time during the school year for all that a resourceful teacher may do to enrich his teaching; that is why the long summer vacations mean so much to him, and why he is willing to sacrifice income in order to have the time. Of course, one can find loafers in teaching as well as in politics or bricklaying, but good colleges are not built by loafers.

All of this should help us to answer the question with which we started—how much time should teachers devote to administrative tasks? The answer, for the college that is trying to allow its faculty members the uninterrupted use of at least fifty hours each week needed for superior work in full-time teaching, must be—very little. In each department there are administrative details, such as the enrollment of students, the selection and ordering of textbooks, the scheduling of hours and rooms for the meeting of classes, the supervision of assistants, the answering of correspondence, and the correlation of the courses offered by the members of the department, which can be looked after best by a departmental chairman or secretary.

Where there are two or more members of a department, the rotation of the chairmanship seems a good way to divide up these burdens. The committees authorized to discuss and make recommendations to the faculty on curriculum, student counseling, research, and the library must of their very nature be composed largely of teachers. When new members are to be added to the staff, the members of the departments most closely concerned should be consulted, and should have some part in the decision, though the final responsibility for choice must rest upon the president, since he is held accountable in the long run for the quality of the faculty and of the educational program. To the extent here suggested, the teaching staff must perform administrative functions; but no further. Any additional committee or administrative duties will encroach upon time and interest which should be devoted to the enrichment of teaching.

But what about the Committees on Admissions, Alumni Relations, Athletics, Catalogue, Community Service, Fraternities, Postwar Planning, Public Occasions, Religious Life, Social Program, Student Aid, Student Discipline, Student Publications, Placement, etc., which ordinarily take so much of the time of the average college faculty? An occasional teacher may have special knowledge or experience which will make him a valuable member of one of these committees, but it should be remembered that to the extent that he gives his time to this work he is an administrative officer of the college, and not a teacher; adjustments in teaching load should accordingly be made.

Within the area of teaching itself, the administrative officer is constantly faced by the specter of "academic freedom." The function of the administration is to protect the teacher in his rights and privileges—but also to protect the college, its students, and society against the abuse of these privileges. Differences in teaching method, freedom of thought and presentation within the content of the field, individuality of philosophy, even lapses into anecdotage may all be reasonably practiced by the faculty and defended by the administration; but gross departures from the subject matter of the course to inject personal prejudices or propaganda not in line with one's responsibilities cannot be defended on any ground. President Lotus D. Coffman of the University of Minnesota, in his 1936 report to the people of Minnesota, made a memorable statement on academic liberty: "Nothing is more precious to a university than academic liberty, which is the freedom to carry forward its work. Without it a university cannot survive.

"And yet in common with every other noble virtue or possession of the race, its value is only relative. The abuse of it becomes a vice. Intolerance may masquerade behind its mask. The champions of academic liberty may destroy it by espousing uncritically every new proposal that may be made. Universities cannot chase after every Pied Piper who comes playing down their streets and at the same time be true to their purpose. New ideas must be tested. Time shows that most of them are wrong. A certain lag is desirable for the examination and analysis of new ideas if there is to be real growth and continuity and stability. Universities are the best institutions yet devised by men for the testing of human experience.

"Because knowledge is of common interest, regardless of the political boundaries that separate people, civilized societies and nations generally have given the scholar and the scientist a certain immunity from interference in their search for truth. Such immunity carries with it an obligation. Alas, while the claim to immunity is rarely forgotten, the accompanying obligation too often is. Using the shield of 'academic liberty' for protection, faculty representatives occasionally become the advocates of programs, of causes, of movements which bear no relation to the fields of learning that they have mastered. The fact that this brings them into disrepute with competent scholars who hold steadfastly to the pursuit of human learning, and that they often become objects of public ridicule, is bad enough, but far worse is the fact that performances of this character often jeopardize the very existence of the university itself. . . .

"The universities of this country are in imminent danger of losing their independence because of the extreme liberals who intolerantly seek action without knowledge, and because of the ultra-conservatives who are goaded into antagonism when speech is free, even though it is based on knowledge. No virtue can be preserved by abuse. If scholarship gives way to communism or fascism, if it ties itself to emotion, to one-sided social

or economic theories, to any form of propaganda, the privileges
it has so honorably enjoyed will be lost. Human learning will
continue to guide human advancement only if educational
institutions refuse to meddle with, or to be dominated by,
'isms,' creeds, or doctrines. Science cannot be coerced and still
be science; scholarship cannot be prostituted to preconceived
or ulterior ends and still be scholarship."

With the general spirit of President Coffman's statement we
are in complete accord, but the situation is hardly as simple as
is implied by the last few sentences quoted. Science and all
other forms of human learning deal with facts, and facts wherever found should be recognized and accepted as such: but
facts do not carry with them their own interpretation, and it
frequently happens that a given body of facts is capable of
more than one interpretation. This is what creeds and doctrines
are for—to interpret facts and to project interpretations into
many areas of human interest where no facts are available.

Man still stands before the deeper mysteries of life without
any answer that he is intellectually forced to accept—his own
origin and destiny, the purpose of human existence and its
place in the sum total of cosmic existence, the significance of
his ideals of truth, beauty, love, and their validity beyond the
transient reality of his own finite existence, etc.—such questions
and the response they call forth constitute the foundation on
which every form of human society is based. It is here that
ignorance and bigotry are likely to be entrenched and it is here
that learning and enlightenment find their greatest opportunity.

Every nation is founded on assumptions, explicit or implied,
and every individual is a bundle of beliefs of one sort or another. The function of liberal education is not to produce people
who have no convictions or loyalties, nor should liberal arts
colleges "refuse to meddle with, or to be dominated by, 'isms,'
creeds or doctrines," but they should be willing to keep their
beliefs exposed to the light of all available facts and to modify

them when new experiences bring material for fresh interpretations.

Liberally educated people recognize that their understanding of truth is always partial and incomplete and that our scientific formulas and our social and religious doctrines are, therefore, in constant need of revision to make them adequate as expressions of growing knowledge and ever-increasing insight. The recognition of this distinction between truth in itself and our understanding of truth prevents intellectual and spiritual arrogance and enables one who understands the distinction to be tolerant and sympathetic in his relations with those who differ with him in his opinions and attitudes. This spirit of liberal learning is likely to develop a sense of companionship among people of different cultural backgrounds in the search after common modes of thought and ways of actions, on which depend so largely the peace of the world and the happiness of all mankind.

The responsibilities that the freedom of teaching carries with it must be assumed by the teacher himself—they cannot be imposed by the administration. Administrative officers may discuss with teachers criticism of their work and make suggestions, but in the last analysis the teacher must be responsible for his own work—the relationship in a true college can never be one of supervision. The teaching, of course, should be in line with the announced purpose of an institution and there should be a clear understanding as to what limitations this imposes before a teacher is appointed—certainly before he is given a permanent appointment.

What kind of president does a college need? The answer will depend upon the stage of development the college has reached and will vary with the problems it faces. If the finances need strengthening, a man with business capacity and promotional gifts will be required. If the main source of support and students is denominational, a religious leader is the natural choice;

this explains why a large percentage of college presidents have come from the ministry. If finances are reasonably secure, a trained scholar with understanding of educational procedure and ideas about curricular experimentation would be stimulating. If the college has reached a point where faculty retirements or expansion or friction indicate considerable turnover in personnel, a person with deep human sympathies and understanding is needed. If alumni loyalties need strengthening, an outstanding alumnus may be best.

If the faculty itself is a compact, friendly group, running smoothly, perhaps a member of the faculty should be considered. If the tradition, in a woman's college, is to have a woman president, the board should hesitate before changing the policy. Younger men might have the advantage of enthusiasm, of building their lives into a long career at one college or of establishing a brilliant reputation which would lead to a call to a more responsible position; older men often have valuable experience, prestige already established, and contacts with men and women of means and influence, which may be of great help. There is no necessity of limiting the field of choice to professional educators or ministers; successful businessmen, engineers, journalists, surgeons, lawyers, and bankers are now serving as effective college administrators.

A college needs a president who will co-ordinate the various branches and activities of the institution—the business management, to assure that funds are judiciously invested and expended, that the budget is fairly administered to advance the total interests of the educational program, that the plant is properly maintained, and, when new buildings are built, that they are built to fit into the general architectural and developmental plan of the campus; the personnel and counseling services, such as the deans' offices, the admissions office, alumni and publicity directors, directors of student aid, placement offices, athletic and social program directors, to ensure that none works without considering the others; the instructional branch, already discussed; the library, which can be of great service to the instructional program if its staff members are considered by faculty and students alike as educational counselors; and the trustees.

Above all, in times almost certain to be troublous to the human spirit, in days when our American way of life with all its freedoms will be on trial in the court of the world, our colleges need men of faith to guide them and to inspire those whose footsteps may falter. Such a president must have faith not only in himself and in the people associated with him, but in man as a spiritual being, and in God in whose will is our freedom and whose purpose includes all mankind.

The board of trustees of a college is the final legal authority in the institution, and upon its members rests the responsibility for seeing that the purposes of the college's existence are realized. Members of a board should not think of themselves as serving merely in their capacity as individuals, but as representatives of the constituency of the college and of society as a whole. Some of them are elected as representatives of the alumni or the denomination or the state, and should speak for the group that appointed them; but all should consider themselves as holders of a trust given them by the donors to the college, the earlier trustees, the alumni, the faculty past and present, and the student body.

The most important function of trustees is the selection of a president. They should seek advice and the informal cooperation of the faculty, alumni, and perhaps other groups supporting the college; but they should carry unshared the responsibility for the final decision. Having given due consideration to the needs of the institution and the qualifications of candidates, they should elect a chief executive and then give him their support in carrying out the program he presents for their approval. There will be enough destructive criticism from the outside; within the board the spirit should be one of helpfulness. Of course, if the president through sins of commission or omission loses the confidence of his board, the time has come for him to resign. Though he is the defender of academic freedom and permanent tenure, he cannot claim them for himself, for the welfare of the institution is too dependent upon a satisfactory relationship between himself and the constituency. He should be given adequate time to make other arrangements, but no president can carry on without the support of his board.

General policies, tuition charges, budget allocations, appointments of faculty to permanent positions, all should be thoroughly discussed by the board. In the smaller colleges the board members often assume major responsibility for investments; in larger institutions the volume of business is so great that a full-time investment officer must be employed, or the services of a bank engaged. Perhaps the greatest assistance trustees can give to a president is to help him personally in the establishment of contacts with individuals and organizations able to help the college with funds. Adequate financial support is basic. No institution can hope to have a long and worthy future unless this problem can be solved. The president and trustees working together bear this responsibility.

CHAPTER IX

The College and the University

President Hadley of Yale, in one of his annual reports many years ago, said: "The primary object of a university is to establish and maintain high standards of scientific investigation, general culture, and professional training. Its secondary object is to teach as many students as possible in the different lines with which it concerns itself." Similar statements may be found in the publications of many other universities. As contrasted with the object of a university so interpreted, the primary object of a college is to teach and it is concerned not with many lines but with one—those processes which represent the unfolding of the potentialities of the individual student and the disciplines and methods best adapted to bring this about.

The story of American universities, as distinguished from American colleges, may be said to begin with the establishment of Johns Hopkins University in Baltimore in 1873. Its patron bequeathed a fortune of $7,000,000—half to found a hospital, half for a "university" emphasizing graduate and professional studies. Daniel Coit Gilman came from the presidency of the University of California to head this new institution, and gave it immediately immense impetus and prestige. Harvard, Yale, Clark, and Columbia followed suit shortly, and by 1900 the university system was established in America.

It was built largely upon the model of the German universities. Bismarck by 1870 had established the German Empire as the dominant political power on the continent. American scholars began to flock to Germany to prepare themselves to teach in the new American graduate schools. A glance at the faculty roster of any college or university in the United States around 1900 will show that almost all the Ph.D. degrees were from Germany—the doctorate being practically unknown in England. Since that date American universities have trained their own scholars in increasing numbers, and World War I terminated German educational prestige.

Seventy years have produced a magnificent growth of American graduate and professional schools; into them has gone the bulk of the great gifts to American education; there has been something very appealing to philanthropists in this new development. America can be justly proud of its vast university plants and faculties, but she must not forget that, before the university began, and while the graduate and professional schools were achieving their growth, colleges, uniquely American, were founded in every section of the country and their broad, basic teaching has had a profound effect on the thinking and ideals and leadership of the whole nation.

Whereas the influence of the German university was all in the direction of tool subjects and early specialization, the American college has steadily maintained its confidence in liberal education, without narrowing into specialization too early. According to former Chancellor Bruening of Germany, the German citizenry was excellently trained in technical and professional skills, but without the over-all understanding and interest necessary to successful democratic society; in America, the college influence has been largely responsible for maintaining widespread faith in the assumptions and ideals of democracy and has given breadth and perspective to technical and professional training.

The program of a college overlaps with that of a university in only one section of its activities. Practically all universities include colleges of liberal arts, called by various names but answering that general description. On most university campuses the college of largest student enrollment and of most "collegiate" glamour is the undergraduate college of arts and sciences. In many cases, however, it has been so plundered, especially after the first year or two, by the schools of education, engineering, agriculture, home economics, commerce, journalism, mines, etc., that only a handful of students remain to secure their degrees from the arts college.

There are undoubtedly many good colleges on university campuses. This may be a historical circumstance, as in the case of Harvard, Princeton, Yale, Cornell, Brown, or Duke, where the college was well established long before the university came into being. Or it may be a matter of established policy by the trustees, as at Michigan, North Carolina, Northwestern, or Stanford, where the undergraduate program has been of prime concern. In many of the other universities the college is definitely a stepchild and treated as such; even in the most friendly universities the college is struggling against the campus current. Rewards of rank and salary are usually given to the research professors at the graduate level rather than to the unusually effective undergraduate teachers. The graduate departments continue to hold under their control the instructorships and assistantships in the undergraduate classes, to be assigned to promising research students and candidates for the doctorate, often with scant regard to their fitness for teaching.

A faculty member can gauge his advancement through the years by the gradual diminution of undergraduate courses and the increase of those numbered "for graduate students only." Some great scholars, anxious to retain the common touch, have insisted upon keeping one of their courses open to undergraduates so that they may lecture to a good-sized audience, but they have frequently ruined a good idea by carrying the graduate method down into the lower level. Not until the average undergraduate teacher in the college of liberal arts in our universities is secure in the knowledge that his abilities will be recognized and rewarded as soon and as substantially where he is as they will be if he moves into the graduate level—not until then will the university college really attain its birthright. Some universities, because of the manner in which their endowment funds and research funds are designated, find themselves unable to grant this equality.

The independent college, on the other hand, is free to emphasize those aspects of plant, equipment, atmosphere, and faculty which are conducive to the most effective undergraduate life and program. The best buildings are intended for the use of the college student, the equipment is purchased with his needs in mind—not for the benefit of those engaged in advanced research. The college atmosphere predominates because it is the only atmosphere there is. The faculty members are chosen primarily because they are able to teach and have a liking for it, and a real interest in their students. They know that the highest rewards of rank and salary within the gift of the college may be gained by them as teachers; therefore, they will not push away the ignorant questioning freshman because they are bored with his naïveté—they know that the effectiveness of their teaching will be judged by the significance of the changes that take place in the mind of this same freshman.

The student in the liberal arts college will often find himself in elementary classes taught by the head of the department, a full professor with broad and rich experience as a college teacher. Not that college teachers are discouraged from research; many of them carry on important studies, and publish frequently. But they realize that research is not the sine qua non for promotion, and therefore they need not publish unless they have something worth saying.

The responsibilities of graduate schools center in knowledge for its own sake and in the enlargement of its areas. Professional schools are responsible for maintaining and improving the standards of the professions and training practitoners. The concern of the colleges is with students. Research of the type proper to the graduate school could be carried on by the faculty without any student body at all; liberal education without students is a contradiction in terms.

A university, excepting its college, may be compared, in respect to its purpose and the qualifications of its staff, to a symphony orchestra: an orchestra is not concerned with the health or manners or opinions or character of the people who listen to its performances, though there is always the hope that the effect will be beneficial. Its function is to produce music of the greatest possible perfection; so the medicine or the law or the engineering or the historical research of the university must be the best possible—when that is accomplished, the chief ends of the university are attained. The players in the symphony orchestra are chosen because of their outstanding ability in playing their particular instruments; in like manner, the members of a graduate school faculty are selected on the basis of their knowledge of a subject matter field and their ability to carry on significant research in that area. This is likewise true to a great extent of the faculty of the professional schools, though in this area there is need of able teachers also. There is no implication that able teachers and accomplished research workers cannot be combined; there have been shining examples of this combination, but they are rare.

The question is sometimes asked, why should not the liberal arts sections of universities be turned over entirely to the separately organized colleges, leaving the universities free to develop their graduate and professional work? The considerations for maintaining the college within a university are the same as those which may be urged in favor of university affiliations for professional and technical schools—the influences of liberal arts on applied and specialized training. John Henry Newman in one of his distinguished discourses on *The Idea of a University* pointed out the necessity of surrounding scientific research and technical and professional training with the liberal arts if the highest standards in these fields are to be attained: "There will be this distinction as regards a Professor of Law, or of Medicine, or of Geology, or of Political Economy, in a University and out of it, that out of a University he is in danger of being absorbed and narrowed by his pursuit, and of giving Lectures which are the Lectures of nothing more than a lawyer, physician, geologist, or political economist; whereas in a University he will know just where he and his science stand, he has come to it, as it were, from a height, he has taken a survey of all knowledge, he is kept from extravagance by the very rivalry of other studies, he has gained from them a special illumination and largeness of mind and freedom and self-possession, and he treats his own in consequence with a philosophy and a resource, which belongs not to the study itself, but to his liberal education."

Colleges of liberal arts, whether in universities or separately organized, have a common purpose, and the conditions necessary to make their purpose effective are not essentially different in the two situations—teachers interested in students, with salaries sufficient to secure and hold the best, attractive and convenient buildings with adequate equipment, numbers limited in relation to faculty and facilities, a curriculum suited to its purpose, an unhurried program with leisure for meditation, and an atmosphere which is congenial to the ideals and the spirit of liberal learning. Colleges without university affiliations, with limited enrollments, free from the "dwarfing pressure of numbers," have advantages which balance their isolation, while colleges in the midst of the multitude share in the prestige and public recognition that numbers bring.

The separate colleges, in order to provide an environment conducive to intimate personal relations without the constant impact of the city, have for the most part sought the small town, the suburban community, or even the country. Amherst, Bowdoin, Dartmouth, Denison, DePauw, Grinnell, Hamilton, Middlebury, Oberlin, Pomona, Williams, and scores of others have their towns almost to themselves—and Boston or New York, Cleveland, Indianapolis, Des Moines, or Los Angeles is not too far away for an occasional weekend of theater or for metropolitan field studies. Universities, because the medical and law and business and engineering and architectural schools need clinical opportunities for study, have naturally preferred large centers of population as best adapted for their work—the beauties of Ithaca, Ann Arbor, Champaign, and Iowa City notwithstanding. There are admitted advantages in having a college in a "college town" and a university in a metropolis; however, their geographical location is probably not so important as before the days of easy and almost universal transportation.

President Hoover wrote a statement in 1932 which summarizes so well the difference between college and university and the essential function and position of the college in American life that his words will serve as a fitting close to this chapter:

"Colleges were among the first organized undertakings of our Colonial ancestors after their arrival in this country. Our forefathers came in search of religious and political freedom, and it was most natural that they should early create institutions of learning to train religious and political leaders. The American College, as developed from these beginnings, became a characteristic and almost uniquely American institution.

"The rapid development of science, of mechanical industry and of the technology of industrial processes, led to specialization and encouraged the rise of the University. Such valuable results have flowed from this larger and more complex type of institution of learning that the colleges have suffered in esteem.

"No one would wish to discontinue the training of specialists, but it does clearly appear that the older and simpler College, with its emphasis upon rounded culture, still is indispensable to our national life. Its product of well-rounded men and women, their minds stored with a balanced fund of knowledge and their imaginations trained to perceive its relation to normal life and its possibilities of development, still supplies an urgent need, grown perhaps more urgent than ever amid the complexities of modern civilization."

CHAPTER X

Colleges Should Select Their Students

In a postwar population of 150,000,000 Americans, approximately 10,000,000 will be of college age; that is, of the years 18 through 21. How many of these should be in college? In the past fifty years the trend has been steadily upward. In 1890 there were only 156,756 students in all colleges and universities; by 1910 the number had doubled to 355,213; by 1930 there were 1,100,737; in 1940, the last normal year, a peak was reached at 1,494,203. The general population and the size of the age group also had grown during these years, but the ratio of college students to total population had risen from one in 400 in 1890 to one in 266 in 1910, one in 112 in 1930, and one in 88 in 1940, while the percentage of the age group who attended college rose from 3 per cent in 1890 to 4.8 per cent in 1910, 12.4 per cent in 1930, and 15.4 per cent in 1940. Even if we should assume that our total American population is rapidly approaching a plateau, must we also assume that 15 per cent of the age group is the maximum who will attend college?

The Honorable John W. Snyder, in his May 20, 1946, report as director of the Office of War Mobilization, made the following prophecy: "Next year the demand upon the colleges and universities will be even greater, and it will continue to increase until within the next decade it is estimated that about 3,000,000 students—double the prewar enrollment—will be enrolled in college each year. . . . The colleges stand on the threshold of a period of growth comparable to that experienced a generation ago by our high schools. That growth has been speeded by the flood of returning veterans, but it was under way even before the war. Never again will the proportion of our youth seeking education beyond high school be as small as it was before the war. On the contrary, we may expect college and university enrollments to continue to increase and to be double their pre-war size by the mid-1950s."

If Secretary Snyder's prophecy **is** correct, then approximately 30 per cent of the age group will attend college. If the nation and the colleges adopt the policy that all who are mentally able to profit from education beyond the secondary level should receive it, the percentage might eventually rise to 50 per cent. The major deterrent is, of course, financial. If scholarships, loans, and work opportunities from private and state funds made college possible, and the educational demands of industry and agriculture made it desirable, certainly a large number would attend. No limitations seem consistent with the basic principles of American democracy except those imposed by the native ability of students and their willingness to take advantage of opportunities offered. There should be no fixed class lines in the United States, and as President Conant of Harvard has put it in describing the purpose of Harvard's national scholarships, colleges "should let down a ladder" into all geographic, economic, and social levels of our population.

To meet the needs of perhaps 3,000,000 students, all sorts of institutions will be required—large and medium and small, tax-supported and denominationally supported and independent, liberal and technical, junior colleges and four-year colleges, professional schools and universities, men's colleges and women's colleges and coeducational institutions, residential colleges with students in dormitories and city colleges with students living at home, expensive colleges and moderately priced ones and work-as-you-go schools. This situation will make it more important than ever for each institution to formulate its educational objectives and to recognize the limitations of its program and facilities.

It is also important that better methods be devised to guide students to institutions best adapted to serve their needs. For many years past the older eastern colleges, with long established prestige and a large body of loyal alumni who wish to send their children back to their alma mater, have found that their problem is largely one of selection from an abundance of applicants. During the depression there were some difficulties and a lowering of entrance requirements, and there was a repetition of this phenomenon during the war, but in normal peaceful times the task of their directors of admissions has been one of selecting the more desirable.

Among the younger institutions in the rest of the country the past twenty-five years have seen the rise of a competitive promotional system of recruiting which can remind us of nothing short of the impressment of American seamen that led to the War of 1812. The large state universities and other tax-supported institutions have sought numbers in order that they might justify increased appropriations from the legislature; the independent colleges have gone in for heavy promotion because they needed the tuition incomes or they wanted high quality or they hoped to expand into a larger college or a university. In prosperous times there were enough students to go around; in bad times, as from 1930 to 1936, many campuses were half filled, and pressure began to be applied for more promotional literature, larger staffs of field workers, greater financial inducements, and more alluring campus activities. The scholar on the faculty protests when he sees more money being spent on advertising literature than on new books for the library, but the businessman on the board of trustees insists that you cannot market your product without spending a reasonably high per cent on sales promotion.

The director of admissions or dean of new students or assistant to the president in charge of admissions is a new development in college administration, but he has risen so rapidly that he now stands in many institutions second only to the president in strategic importance. Many colleges could easily justify, on a hard cash basis, the payment to a successful director of admissions of a salary considerably higher than that paid to professors or deans. If he has the personality and training required by the position he would probably make a superior teacher, but he also needs the sympathetic understanding of a dean of men plus the cordiality of an alumni secretary and the promotional drive of a money-raiser. He works twelve months in the year, is never sure of success until enrollment is over in the fall, and then begins immediately to worry about prospects for the next year.

So important do some colleges consider the director of admissions that they provide him with a staff of full-time assistants with a salary budget at least one-tenth as large as the entire salary budget for instruction, an ample travel allowance, and offices in the larger cities. One midwestern junior college, with an admissions staff of almost a score, divides the country into as many districts and keeps a full-time salesman in states more than a thousand miles from the campus. All the foregoing seems justified by the fact that no educational institution can operate without students, and the faculty are kept happier if their students are reasonably intelligent.

Under pressure from the admissions departments, faculties have modified the requirements for admissions greatly during the past twenty-five years. Whereas previously it was necessary to be a graduate from a high school, in the college preparatory course, with grades sufficiently high for a recommendation from the principal, and with sixteen credits distributed four in English, four in Latin or a modern language (preferably both), at least two in mathematics, two in science, and two in history, the barriers fell one by one until today a graduate from almost any course with almost any scholastic record is eligible, and some institutions will admit those who have finished the junior or even the sophomore year in high school. Those which admit by examination care not by what process the knowledge was acquired; the "GI Bill," Public Law 346, providing veterans of World War II with a year or more of education at government expense, has undoubtedly served to make entrance requirements even more flexible. On the other hand, the flood of veterans is so great that colleges can be more selective, and standards may be raised.

One development in admissions procedure is certain to see great expansion in the future—the gathering of a complete personnel file on each student before entrance. Into this file will go not only the customary high school transcript and formal application, but also recommendations or analyses from high school teachers, representative alumni of the college, and trained interviewers; a physician's history and certificate of physical ability to pursue a college course; the test results of academic aptitudes, skills in mathematics and English and foreign languages, knowledge or academic achievement in science and literature and fine arts and social studies, personality adjustment inventories, and vocational interests of many sorts. All these go to make up a student's "profile," which is unique and must be analyzed by an admissions officer to decide whether the student should be admitted; after admission, the profile is useful to the guidance officer to serve as a basis for suggesting a course of study.

The director of admissions and his committee, in selecting the students to be admitted, should consider both the students' qualifications and the institution's abilities to meet them. Not every student who should be encouraged to continue his training beyond high school should be directed to a four-year college of liberal arts. Probably not more than from fifteen to twenty per cent of any age group have the type of mental ability required. A liberal arts college might well describe in specific terms the type of student who will be admitted. The purpose of such a college centers in the full-rounded development of a comparatively few carefully selected students of a certain type to be found at all social and financial levels of society. These students should be of more than average ability and might be expected to rank in the upper half of their high school or preparatory school graduating class.

In addition they might be expected to have a sense of purpose in their education which fitted in definitely with a liberal arts program; that is, no specific, vocational, or technical training to be secured during the undergraduate years, but a general education plus such liberal studies as are necessary for highest personal development. The chief handicap of four-year colleges during the past twenty-five years has been the difficulty of finding students properly qualified by native ability, previous training, and social attitude to profit by what they have to offer. The result has been that colleges generally have accepted large numbers of students who are not really interested in their work and who make no worth-while use of the opportunities provided. The future of four-year colleges should involve more definite restrictions upon entering students, leaving to other types of institutions, better adapted for the purpose, the responsibility of providing opportunities for those who are not qualified to do college work.

From the standpoint of what a liberal arts college is for—its purpose—the most discouraging circumstance is the fact that less than half of those who enter as freshmen continue until graduation. Today the average college must admit 225 freshmen yearly to keep a student body of 600, for by the sophomore year only 175 are left, and in the last two years only 100 each. If students could be more carefully selected before entrance to be sure they want and can profit from what the college offers; if the quality of counseling and instruction could be so adapted that the individual feels that his needs are being met; if graduation from college could be made as attractive to the sophomore as going to college was to the high school senior—

then the four classes might be kept at more nearly equal size and the college would be more likely to see its purpose accomplished in the lives of its students.

The serious problem of competition for student enrollments would come much nearer solution if the colleges would face the facts of student supply with candor and adjust their ideas of size accordingly. All our institutions cannot expand indefinitely. Colleges of liberal arts in particular should limit their numbers. The ideal size for such an institution is probably somewhat smaller than the maximum it has attained. Many colleges should improve and stabilize their programs by reducing their student bodies instead of seeking to expand and spread an inadequate endowment income over an enlarged faculty and plant.

No matter how many students may be going to college by 1950, there will always be competition to secure those of high scholastic ability and talents in various extracurricular fields. To attract these men and women and to make college possible for those of limited means, aid funds have been established by individual colleges, by states, as in the case of New York, and by other agencies. The amount of financial assistance may vary from a small honor scholarship of a token amount to the entire expense for all four years. Some of them are awarded as prizes on the basis of competition or as a reward for high scholastic attainment in high school or college. These are justifiably called scholarships.

Many of them are endowed as memorials, and the income can be used only for this purpose. Many students who need help and are eminently deserving prospective citizens do not rank in the top ten per cent of their class; for them the colleges provide "grants-in-aid," usually somewhat less in amount than the scholarships and awarded primarily upon the basis of proved need combined with satisfactory grades. Colleges must be chary of the number and amount of grants-in-aid awarded, for usually these sums must come from current income rather than from specifically endowed scholarship funds.

In place of grants, or in addition to them, students can be given opportunities to work, such as waiting on tables for their meals, jobs on the campus, etc. They can also be helped to find part-time employment in the community. It should be recognized, however, that much time spent in employment, accepted only for the purpose of earning money, is likely to interfere with the main purpose for which the student is in college, and will probably deprive him of many advantages which he would otherwise gain from his college experience. College opportunities are made possible only at great cost. If the student is prevented from taking full advantage of them by the necessity of earning money during the college year, society is probably the loser. In other words, the value of the money he earns is probably less than what is lost by the partial use he makes of the opportunities provided.

It is for this reason that many colleges have acquired substantial loan funds which are available to juniors and seniors at a low rate of interest and are repayable upon convenient terms after graduation. If these loans are carefully assigned and retired regularly in accordance with agreed-upon schedules of repayment, a loan fund can rotate rapidly and make it possible for hundreds of students to secure an education. The securing of a college loan has developed in many a student a sense of financial responsibility and independence and has enabled him to devote his entire time to his studies during college, paying off the loan when his earning powers are greater. It is embarrassing to many students and their parents to produce proof of need of an outright gift. It is equally embarrassing to the college to refuse it or to grant it when it is not needed. Credit, however, can be established and maintained to the benefit of both college and student.

Most colleges are now busily at work trying to increase their endowed scholarship and grant funds. There is also considerable agitation among the various states and in Congress for the establishment of scholarships to be given to students by the state itself and possibly by the national government. The aid at present given to veterans sets a pattern which will probably have great influence in the future. The Navy has already established naval ROTC units on 52 campuses, where the full tuition, room, and board of the student will be paid for by the Navy during his entire four-year program.

There is, however, a requirement that the student agree to put in a certain period of time in active service in the Navy following his training. The Army, in setting up its ROTC program, is expecting to use a great many more colleges and to give more financial assistance than was granted to those who took ROTC training before the war. These two ROTC programs may make it possible for more than 100,000 students to remain in college each year with most of their expenses paid. Many denominations have established funds for scholarships and loans to young people in the church who wish to go on for college training. Insurance companies have urged parents to establish endowment policies which will pay for tuition and college expense for their children and have arranged for loans on such policies for students wishing to attend college.

There are also some independent loan funds, such as the Henry Strong Foundation of Chicago, which make loans to deserving students on several college campuses and allow them to be repaid on generous terms during the years after graduation. It would seem, therefore, that the movement is all in the direction of greater financial assistance to students, and it should be quite possible for a high percentage of the students applying for college admission in the future to see their way through to graduation.

CHAPTER XI

Students Become Alumni

"By their fruits ye shall know them" is certainly true of the colleges. Studies recently made by Who's Who in America reveal that in the past decade from 86 to 89 per cent of the noted and distinguished men and women of this country have attended college, most of them being graduates. In the 1944–45 edition, 32,153 of the 33,893 people listed furnished general educational data. Of this number 8,368 had earned a doctor's degree, 4,603 the master's degree, and 10,961 the bachelor's degree, or a total of 74.44 per cent with degrees; in addition, 4,605 had attended college but had not been graduated, bringing the percentage of college trained people to 88.76 per cent. The 1946–47 edition of Who's Who does not make such a study for the whole group but studies only the 8,919 new names included in this edition. Of this latter group 88.62 per cent attended college, so that the average is almost identical with that of the earlier account.

It can be argued that inclusion in Who's Who is no guarantee of quality, for a number of people are included quite arbitrarily, such as federal judges, judges of the highest appellate jurisdiction in states and territories, attorneys general, heads of the larger universities and colleges, heads of the leading societies devoted to educational and scientific aims, bishops and chief ecclesiastics of all the larger religious denominations, and others for whom graduation from college is almost an absolute prerequisite. Nevertheless, Who's Who provides perhaps the most reliable standard for judging the accomplishments of our contemporaries. Naturally the older colleges and universities have produced the larger numbers, but the newer institutions are creeping up as their graduates reach the age when they are likely to be considered for listing. When the percentage of living graduates is considered rather than the gross numbers, the smaller colleges like Amherst and Hampden-Sydney top the list.

A recent study by Professor B. W. Kunkel of Lafayette College of the 13,633 persons included in the Dictionary of American Biography shows a somewhat different picture, because no living persons are included and the study covers all American history from the sixteenth century on. The study reveals that of those born before 1800 only about 25 per cent were college graduates, but the percentage has risen decade by decade until 75 per cent of those born 1880–90 were graduated—approximately the same per cent as in Who's Who.

As might be expected, Harvard leads with 720 graduates spread through its three hundred years of history, and Yale follows with 552; but it is significant that of the top twelve institutions five are colleges rather than universities—Dartmouth, Union, Amherst, Williams, and Bowdoin. Here, again, it might be argued that naturally generals are graduates of West Point and admirals of Annapolis, that all outstanding physicians and surgeons and ministers and educators who get into such a collection must attend a college to enter their professions, but the fact still remains that the judgment of history must be accepted as a hallmark of quality. We can, therefore, draw the conclusion that a college education is a potent help to a man or woman eager to reach the heights in America.

Our colleges must never forget that students do become alumni, and the best advertisement a college can put out is a loyal alumnus. In the next generation he will send his children to the place where he was happy; she will talk to her friends about going or sending their children; they will contribute to the alumni fund and eventually to the endowment. But the college must not look upon its alumni merely as possible contributors of students or money; it must seek to help every alumnus to find his proper place in society, to keep him interested in continuing with his education formally or informally, to serve him in every way that it is possible for an educational institution to serve. The college does not stop giving at graduation. It continues to give throughout life. For some alumni their college is as vital to them in middle or old age as it was when they were freshmen—perhaps more so, for now they see what it is all about.

It is pleasant to be told by *Time* magazine that college graduates receive incomes of twice the average size, that two-thirds of all families with incomes of more than three thousand dollars are college families, and that holders of liberal arts degrees earn quite as much as those with specialized training. But the satisfactions of civilized life are not all financial; we would rather know that our graduates are living happier, fuller lives, more helpful to others, because they once lived in the formative influence of our campus and have continued to enjoy the benefits of that college association. The real purpose of a college finds its fulfillment in the lives of its graduates—their ideals, attitudes, and influence, and the quality and spirit of their work.

The graduates of a college should share in the determination of its policies. Alumni frequently have a legal connection with their alma mater by being permitted to nominate or elect a limited number of alumni trustees to the board. The process of election, if it is democratic and spread over a sufficiently large percentage of the graduate group, is a stimulus to interest in the college. There is, of course, the danger that as vacancies occur in the regular membership of the board only those who have previously served as alumni trustees will be considered, and eventually the entire board will be composed of alumni. Such a situation may lead to unwarranted self-satisfaction, narrowness of point of view, and lack of perspective; most college boards seek to protect themselves from too much institutional inbreeding by deliberately bringing in nonalumni as members.

Another method of developing alumni interest and responsibility is to set up committees advisory to the board on each of the main departments of the college and to appoint influential alumni and nonalumni to these committees. For example, the advisory committee for the chemistry department might well consist of some outstanding chemical engineers or manufacturers, some physicians, some high school and university teachers of chemistry, and some research chemists from industry or the foundations; among these might be several alumni, who would thus serve their college in the field where they are best qualified. On these committees would undoubtedly appear excellent candidates for later election to the board of trustees, and their previous service would make them doubly valuable.

There is a tradition among colleges and universities that the only topic upon which alumni will really grow enthusiastic is intercollegiate athletics. There can be no doubt that alumni, whether or not they themselves participated in intercollegiate competition, enjoy watching the teams representing their colleges compete athletically. The games played on the campus serve to bring them back and to renew their interest; those played at a distance, if they are judiciously located, also can serve to bring alumni groups together. Here the danger is that alumni naturally want to see their college teams win a large percentage of the games and will begin to exert pressure on the administration to award "athletic scholarships" to outstanding high school players, to lower the academic standards so that these students can be admitted and kept eligible for competition, and to appoint a coach who will "turn out" winning teams.

The Carnegie Foundation for the Advancement of Teaching, in its famous 1929 report, pointed out the growing allurements of large gate receipts, especially for colleges and universities in metropolitan areas. That this danger is not diminishing is shown by the fact that the attendance at athletic contests in the first years following World War II has been greater than ever before in American history. The Carnegie report also indicated that whereas many institutions preserve a strictly amateur and nonsubsidizing attitude toward the athletes on their campus, the evil often lies in the surreptitious action of individual alumni who see to it that prominent athletes get through their college with all expenses paid. It will probably be increasingly difficult for colleges of high standing to support a program of athletics which will please the alumni and the public and at the same time be beneficial to the students.

The direct services of a college to its alumni are normally rendered through an alumni association, with a secretary located on the campus. This association office keeps an up-to-date file of the names and addresses of all who have ever attended the college, and serves to keep the alumni informed of activities at the college and among their friends. Some institutions require that alumni pay annual dues if they are to receive the news bulletins and magazines, but the wiser policy would seem to be to render such services without charge and to depend indirectly upon the good will so created to support the enterprise. Every graduate is naturally interested in hearing what has happened to the friends and acquaintances he had in college; therefore, the staple contents of the alumni magazine should be "class notes," with second place for news of current happenings on the campus, a third place for educational or service features, such as articles on recent advances in the fields of the curriculum written by members of the faculty, and only a minor role for the promotion of financial or other activities of the college administration.

The college calendar offers several events each year which should serve as reminders and attractions to alumni. Athletic contests, particularly the "homecoming" football game, stand high in the list in drawing power. Founder's Day, if duly planned with a dinner and program, serves to recall the original and continuing purposes of the college. Regional alumni gatherings in New York, Chicago, Los Angeles, or wherever else there are concentrations of graduates, provide suitable occasions for the president or his delegate to tell what is happening to alma mater. The commencement period, traditionally sacred to the graduating senior, has grown into the time of class reunions and visits to the campus. It is the right and duty of the college to encourage such social gatherings, for the members of a college class in four years build up a family solidarity which should not be allowed to perish for lack of cultivation and renewal.

Some alumni, however, feel that these returns to the old scene should not be merely hilarious; they have asked the faculty to provide an "alumni college" of refresher courses, lasting as much as a week in such elaborate programs as those of the University of Chicago and Smith College. These recognize the fact that liberal education is not a static affair, but needs to be brought up to date at frequent intervals. Therefore, continuation centers following the alumni college pattern may furnish the answer to the problem of the college's relations to the community and to its alumni. Liberal arts colleges have a responsibility to see to it that their alumni are carrying the ideals of liberal education into public life in the same way that professional schools should study ways in which their alumni are influencing the standards and accomplishments of the professions.

Even the strictly undergraduate liberal arts college needs to give serious consideration to programs of adult education, either through extension courses by mail or through short courses provided on the campus, or by traveling panels of faculty members in the regions served by the college. Adult education has been greatly stimulated by wartime activities and by the provisions of the GI Bill. Many colleges which have never before had evening classes or extension centers are now entering into this field with vigor. Certainly we are never too old to learn, either the colleges or the alumni. The four years of college residence should be merely the beginning of a lifetime relationship to liberal education for all students, with the college continuing to serve as the fountainhead of inspiration and instruction.

CHAPTER XII

How Much Money Does a College Need?

This question would have little meaning if applied to a university. There is no limit to the amount of money a university can put to good use, and its services to its community and state and to the world are limited only by the funds available. Its possible usefulness extends into every area of human interest and welfare, and society receives rich returns for all the money invested—returns in better living conditions, in discoveries which have led to more efficient methods in agriculture, commerce and industry, in researches which have resulted in alleviation of human suffering and in marked extension of human life, and in many other ways.

As compared with such an extensive and varied program, the program of a college of liberal arts is definitely limited, and the amount of money required to enable it to fulfill its purpose can be closely estimated. If a college limits its enrollment and establishes a scale of salaries to be paid, it is possible to determine within narrow margins the amount of money it should have to do its work properly.

In the following pages an attempt is made to outline the financial needs of a college for one thousand students. It is not to be assumed that any number can be fixed as representing the ideal size of a college. Its effectiveness is more dependent upon certain internal relationships, for example, the ratio of teachers to students and the resulting size of classes, than upon the total number enrolled. If funds can be secured to maintain these internal relationships in accordance with high standards, there seems to be no reason why a college of twelve hundred, or even larger, cannot be as effective as an institution of three hundred or five hundred.

In the following statement of needs there is included the estimated expense (without extravagance) of all the essential features a good college should have. Most colleges are admirably equipped in some one department or they have one or two good buildings among a half dozen poor ones. It would probably be difficult to find a college that does not have at least one or two superior teachers on its faculty. But among the hundreds of American colleges comparatively few are fully equipped and properly staffed for the program they attempt to carry. The recommendations here made are not intended to discourage institutions with limited means but to indicate to their supporting constituency what is needed to make their work effective.

It is assumed that the college we are picturing will limit not only its enrollment but also the scope of its work and that it will not attempt to offer graduate opportunities or training in professional or technical fields. It will seek chiefly to meet the needs of those who desire a full four-year course in liberal arts as a preparation for later professional study and life work. With proper care in selecting its students such a college should graduate at least two-thirds of those who enter and would have an actual enrollment approximately as follows: 320 freshmen, 250 sophomores, 215 juniors, and 215 seniors. The biggest gap will be between the freshman and sophomore years, as those who are not able to do satisfactory work will not be encouraged to continue beyond the first year.

It is proposed to offer substantial financial help to students of ability who are not able to pay the regular fees. Perhaps as many as 40 per cent should receive some assistance. However, a sum for this purpose equal to 20 per cent of the total tuition receipts would seem reasonably satisfactory, and it is assumed that one-quarter of this help will be in the form of loans.

A college such as we have in mind will wish to maintain high academic standards. Only students of good ability who are able to meet the regular entrance requirements will be admitted. They will not be permitted, except in special cases, to carry more than sixteen hours of classwork a week, it being deemed more profitable to a student to do work of superior quality than to take more subjects with mediocre success. The size of classes will vary with the level and form of instruction— lecture, discussion, laboratory, seminar, or tutorial. There should be a ratio of not more than twelve students per teacher, which will make it possible to limit the size of classes in each department to such numbers as experience and careful studies indicate as desirable. This ratio will also make possible a moderate teaching load for every instructor, giving him time to become acquainted with each student and enabling him to keep his own intellectual life fresh and vigorous by scholarly achievements on his own account.

The faculty should include a reasonable proportion of mature and experienced teachers; therefore, at least 40 per cent should qualify for the top rank and salary of full professors. The average salary of this group should be not less than $5,000 a year. The range might be from $4,000 to $6,000, with even higher salaries in exceptional cases in recognition of distinguished service in this or other institutions. Three lower ranks are suggested, evenly balanced as to numbers (20 per cent each) and with salaries as follows: associate professors from $3,200 to $4,200, averaging $3,600; assistant professors from $2,600 to $3,600, averaging $3,000; and instructors from $1,800 to $2,800, averaging $2,400. No one will be employed in the work of teaching whose rank or salary is below that of an instructor, fully recognized as a member of the faculty. However, assistants can be used in some departments to good advantage without sharing in the actual work of instruction. The following table represents an example of how the salaries suggested could be distributed in the different ranks:

Professors	Associate Professors	Assistant Professors	Instructors
2 at $6,000	1 at $4,200	1 at $3,600	4 at $2,800
4 at $5,600	2 at $4,000	2 at $3,400	4 at $2,600
6 at $5,200	3 at $3,800	2 at $3,200	3 at $2,400
11 at $5,000	4 at $3,600	5 at $3,000	2 at $2,200
5 at $4,800	4 at $3,400	5 at $2,800	2 at $2,000
2 at $4,500	3 at $3,200	2 at $2,600	2 at $1,800
2 at $4,200			
2 at $4,000			
Average 34 at $5,000	17 at $3,600	17 at $3,000	17 at $2,400

Summary

Rank	Number	%	Average	Amount Paid
Professors	34	40	$5,000	$170,000
Associate Professors	17	20	$3,600	61,200
Assistant Professors	17	20	$3,000	51,000
Instructors	17	20	$2,400	40,800
	85	100	$3,800	$323,000

A system of sabbatical furloughs for full professors equivalent to one year in seven on half pay is recommended. Such a plan should not be strictly administered. It may be desirable for a professor, after six years of service, to take a furlough of one semester on full pay, or he may prefer some other arrangement that would come within the financial possibilities of the general plan. It is of course desirable to offer such furloughs to associate professors and even to those of lower rank, and such arrangements will undoubtedly be made in special cases. However, this will require additional funds.

Another reason for limiting the plan as suggested is that it is assumed that only full professors are on permanent appointment and that all others are appointed for definitely limited periods subject to renewal at the discretion of the college. If a college is able to keep its full professors permanently, it would seem desirable that there be steady but not too rapid changes in all the other ranks either by promotion or by transfer to some other institution. In any case a sabbatical furlough should not be regarded as compensation for service rendered nor as a vacation but as an opportunity to prepare for more effective teaching in the years to follow. Such preparation might well include some important piece of research in a well-equipped university offering opportunities not available in a college.

The following table represents the fields of study ordinarily included in the program of a coeducational liberal arts college and suggests a balanced distribution of teachers of the different ranks. Colleges for men generally include more teachers in science and in some cases in engineering and fewer in the fine arts, while colleges for women have fewer in the sciences and more in social studies and the fine arts and in some cases in home economics. It is assumed that teachers of maturity and experience are more needed in subjects where interpretations are required than in those where the aim is chiefly to find facts or to acquire facilities. A larger percentage of full professors is, therefore, assigned in social studies than in the sciences, and the largest of all in philosophy and religion.

In addition to salaries for teachers, the educational budget will include the salaries of the library staff and administrative officers. The salary of the president should be regarded as expense of that office and not as personal compensation to him. So much depends upon his competence and devotion and his effectiveness is so greatly enhanced when he feels secure in his personal finances that the question of his salary is comparatively unimportant when regarded in the light of the opportunities his office brings him to serve the institution. Except the president, no administrative officer should be thought of in terms of greater recognition or higher salary than a full pro-

	Prof.	Assoc. P.	Asst. P	Instr.	Total
HUMANITIES					
Literature & Philosophy					
English (Literature, Rhetoric, and Speech)	3	3	2	2	10
Classical Languages	1			1	2
Modern Languages	3	2	2	2	9
Philosophy	2				2
Religion	2				2
Fine Arts					
Music	2	2	1	2	7
Art	1	1	1	1	4
Dramatic Arts	1		1		2
	15	8	7	8	38
SOCIAL STUDIES					
History	3	2	1		6
Political Science	1	1			2
Economics	2	1	1		4
Sociology	1	1			2
Psychology	1	1	1		3
Education	1	1			2
	9	7	3	0	19
SCIENCES					
Mathematics	1	1	1	1	4
Astronomy	1				1
Physics	1		1	1	3
Chemistry	2		1	2	5
Geology and Geography ..	1		1	1	3
Biology (Zoology and Botany)	2	1	1	1	5
	8	2	5	6	21
HYGIENE AND PHYSICAL EDUCATION	2		2	3	7
	34	17	17	17	85

fessor.\We have, therefore, included the salaries of the librarian, the dean of the college, dean of women, registrar and director of personnel, director of admissions, and the business manager on the same basis as full professors—an average of $5,000. The salaries of other administrative officers, assistants, secretaries, etc., are estimated in terms of prevailing rates in comparable positions in other fields of employment.

In cases where administrative officers, such as deans or registrars, also offer instruction, a corresponding portion of their salaries should be charged to salaries for teaching, and when regular administrative duties are assigned to teachers a corresponding portion of their salaries should be charged to administration salaries.

Provision should be made for suitable retiring allowances for all college employees. A satisfactory plan will require each year at least 11 per cent of the total salaries of those included. As related to teachers, it is proposed to make the plan optional for instructors and obligatory upon all holding higher ranks. There is included in the salary budget 8 per cent of the total for instructional salaries (exclusive of assistants, who are not eligible for these benefits) and of all salaries for library staff and educational administration. Each beneficiary will be required to set aside each year not less than 3 per cent of his salary in addition to the 8 per cent provided by the college. If any plan is adopted which requires more than 11 per cent, it is expected that the additional amount will be paid by the beneficiary.

The annual payment of 8 per cent by the college is part of the employee's compensation for a given year and should be included in the regular salary budget. The college should, in no case, retain any jurisdiction over the accumulations resulting from this annual 8 per cent payment. It belongs to the employee on the basis of service rendered and should be recognized as his property without any restrictions whatever except that the sum so provided may not be drawn upon for any other purpose during his lifetime.

In inaugurating a pension plan, colleges should be slow in assuming any responsibility for "accrued liabilities." In any case, expense for this purpose should not be included in the current educational budget. Any such provision, together with any pensions actually paid by the college to retired teachers or other staff members, should be included in the noneducational section of the budget. Special gifts (not included in this study) will be necessary to provide for this expense and should be secured before any definite promises are made.

Most colleges will probably wish to sponsor for their employees some plan for group insurance (to expire upon retirement) and for accident and sickness benefits. When these plans are put in operation it is generally expected that the employees will pay the cost. However, experience indicates that this is usually not the case. We have, therefore, included in the proposed salary budget a moderate sum for this purpose. Payments for liability insurance may be regarded as protecting the institution against legal claims and may, therefore, be classified as administration expense rather than as related to salaries.

On the basis of the above recommendations, the salary budget for a college of one thousand students would be approximately as follows in the table on page 136.

It is much more difficult to outline the details of a college plant than of a college faculty. Much depends upon the taste of those in charge, upon local circumstances, including the topography of the campus, and upon other conditions, such as climate in the section of the country in which the college is located. Owing to these variables and contingencies, it is practically impossible to describe a model college plant that will constitute the best solution of the building problems for more than a single institution.

The following table does not include dormitories, dining halls, heating plant, nor any other self-supporting buildings or equipment, such as college hospital, faculty houses, janitors' houses, college bookstore, laundry, farm. These service buildings and equipment should be self-supporting, including proper

For Instruction
　Faculty Members (see page 131) $323,000
　Assistants .... 3,000　　$326,000.00
For Library
　Librarian .... $ 5,000
　Assistants and Secretarial Help ...... 13,000　'$ 18,000.00
For Administration
　President ($12,000 in cash plus house
　　rent and allowance for maintenance) $ 15,000
　Dean of the College, Dean of Women,
　　Registrar and Director of Personnel,
　　Director of Admissions, and Business
　　Manager, receiving an average of
　　$5,000 each 25,000
　Assistants and Secretarial Help ...... 25,000　$ 65,000.00
Total for Salaries $409,000.00
8 per cent allowance for pensions .... 32,480.00°
Allowance for group insurance, sickness
　and accident benefits 3,436.67
Reserve for professors on furlough (½ of
　salaries of active full professors) .... 12,083.33°°
　　　　　　　　　　　　　　　　　　　　　　　$457,000.00

° This sum represents 8 per cent of the total for salaries, exclusive of salaries of assistants in instruction who are not eligible for these benefits. The salaries of visiting professors to take the place of those on furlough are included on the assumption that professors on furlough will receive their full pension allowance in addition to their furlough salary.

°° It is assumed that five full professors will be absent each year. The reserve for furloughs is, therefore, based on $145,000 which active full professors receive.

charges for interest on the investment and for depreciation, and a reasonable reserve set aside each year for retiring the investment. When this plan is followed, no gifts are required for the construction or maintenance of these service properties. If gifts are secured for such properties they could be regarded as endowment invested in these income-producing properties, or, if not so regarded, the gifts could be so applied that the amount of endowment otherwise needed could be correspondingly reduced.

It is not implied that the buildings indicated could be constructed at the present time for the sums suggested. Present prices are so uncertain that estimates based on them would give a distorted picture of the usual college plant requirements. However, in submitting these suggestions we do not have in mind primarily those who are interested in building a new college, but those who desire to develop their present properties into a well-rounded college plant. In presenting the needs for new buildings and equipment to prospective donors, the cost of present buildings will be averaged in with the cost of those still needed, and the total will probably not be far from what is indicated in the table below and at the top of the following page:

EDUCATIONAL PLANT

Grounds

Campus, including grading, paving, drainage system, etc.	$200,000	
Men's Athletic Field	30,000	
Women's Athletic Field	20,000	
		$ 250,000

Educational Buildings

Main Building (recitation rooms, offices for faculty, administration, etc.)	$750,000	
Library Building with seminar rooms (space for 200,000 volumes)	400,000	
Chapel-Auditorium	300,000	
Fine Arts Building, containing theater, music recital hall, art studios, museum galleries, practice rooms, and class rooms	500,000	
Building for Astronomy and Physics	250,000	
Chemistry Building	250,000	
Building for Biology (including greenhouse, etc.) and Geology	250,000	
Stadium, Men's Gymnasium, Swimming Pool, and Field House	350,000	
Women's Gymnasium and Swimming Pool	250,000	
Student Union	200,000	
		$3,500,000

EDUCATIONAL PLANT—*Continued*

Educational Equipment

Library	$400,000	
Laboratory apparatus	250,000	
Art and Music equipment and Museum	250,000	
Gymnasium equipment	75,000	
Chapel equipment (organ, etc.)	40,000	
Furniture, fixtures, office equipment, etc. ...	235,000	
		$1,250,000
Total Value of Educational Plant		$5,000,000

The foregoing recommendations would result in current expenses for educational purposes approximately as follows:

Salaries (see page 136)		$457,000.00
Supplies and Expenses		
Departmental	$25,000	
Library (exclusive of new books and maintenance of building)	3,000	
Administration	20,000	48,000.00
Religious Services and other public occasions		5,000.00
Operation and maintenance of Educational Plant		
Wages	$22,000	
Heat, light, power and water	40,000	
Insurance	10,000	
Repairs and supplies	23,000	
Campus Upkeep	5,000	
		100,000.00
		$610,000.00

From the above it is clear that approximately $600 a year for each student is required to provide for the necessary expenses for directly educational purposes. It is assumed that the income to meet this expense will come from two sources: (1) student tuition fees and (2) income from endowment. The college will not be obliged to ask for gifts for its current educational work.

A tuition fee of $400 is suggested. This is low for eastern colleges, high for western, but a good medium for the stronger colleges of the whole country. This would provide an income of $400,000 if it was all received in cash. However, it is proposed to assist students to the extent of 20 per cent of the total tuition receipts and that three-quarters of this amount will be given in the form of scholarships or grants-in-aid and one-quarter in student loans.

The following table indicates the proposed sources of current income for educational purposes:

Current Educational Income

800 students each paying $400 tuition in cash .	$320,000
150 students each paying $400 tuition with money received as scholarships	60,000
50 students each paying $400 tuition with money received as loans	20,000
	$400,000
Income from Endowment	200,000
Total Educational Income	$600,000

On the basis of the standards indicated above, a college for one thousand students, with a tuition charge of $400, needs $5,000,000 endowment to provide, at 4 per cent, the needed $200,000 to balance the current educational budget. An endowment of $1,500,000 more will be needed to provide $60,000 a year for scholarships and grants-in-aid; also an additional sum of $100,000 to be used as a revolving fund for loans to students. This will make possible student loans amounting to $20,000 a year averaging five years in length, loans ordinarily to be made only to juniors and seniors. It is assumed that any money which students may earn by working during the college year will be used for board and room or for such personal expenses as books, etc., and is not here listed as a source of income.

Regularly recurring annual needs for new books, new laboratory apparatus, and other permanent equipment must be met; permanent improvements or extensions to buildings are frequently necessary. Such expenditures should not be included in the current budget; they represent capital investments. An endowment of $1,500,000 would provide $60,000 a year for such purposes.

A fund of $100,000 to be used as current working capital also is proposed. A college frequently needs to borrow money for short periods of time to take care of some item of prepaid expense, such as insurance, or to finance some undertaking temporarily in anticipation of expected income. This current fund of $100,000 is intended for such purposes, and when not so needed may be invested in productive securities, the income from which would be available for current expenses. This would provide a small annual income for extra expenses not included in the budget.

It is assumed that endowment funds will never be drawn upon for current expenses nor for additions to the educational plant or equipment, and that no endowment securities will ever be used as collateral for loans.

For summary of recommendations see pages 142 and 143.

The current operating budget of a college includes three sections—educational, auxiliary, and noneducational. So far we have discussed only the budget for educational expense. The most important items of expense for auxiliary purposes are the following:

1. College Activities. The costs of such auxiliary activities as intercollegiate athletics, debating, band, orchestra, plays, dances, and student publications are usually cared for by a special fee, collected of all students by the college, administered by a student-faculty committee, with expenses audited regularly. The expense for intercollegiate athletics will include only such costs as those of arranging games, equipping teams, traveling, publicity, and officials. The expense for maintenance of gymnasiums, stadiums, and athletic fields and for salaries

for all coaches and instructors in physical education is regarded as part of the regular budget for educational purposes.

2. Public Concerts, Lectures, etc. These should be self-supporting. If a deficit is likely to occur, this should be made up beforehand by special gifts from those who are willing to act as guarantors. Departmental lectures, designed for groups of students, are regarded as part of the work of instruction, and are included under "departmental expenses."

3. Dormitories and Dining Halls. Colleges, not being charitable institutions, are under no obligation to provide room and board for less than cost. When gifts are used for this purpose, a corresponding reduction in the quality of the distinctly educational work is inevitable, usually in the form of lower salaries to teachers than could otherwise be paid. The fundamental question of policy for a college board of trustees to decide regarding these service properties is whether it is practical and desirable to manage them on a self-supporting basis. This must include a fair income on the total amount invested and a proportionate amount set aside each year in a funded reserve for depreciation, if the investments represent gifts, or for retiring the investments within the lifetime of the properties, if no gifts are involved. If these properties are paid for by gifts, it is comparatively unimportant whether or not they are regarded as endowment. In any case, if managed on a self-supporting plan, they provide a steady and dependable income for the support of the educational program. It is more likely that efficient management will result if such properties are regarded as endowment entitled to a fair income rather than as representing the benevolence of a donor with no expectation that net income on the investment be produced. It is more conservative to arrange with the prospective donor of money for a dormitory to give it for endowment with the understanding that it be invested in a dormitory than to have the money given

BALANCE SHEET—JUNE 30, 1947

ASSETS

Current Funds Assets:

Cash in Banks	$ 22,000	
Accounts Receivable	3,000	
Prepaid Expense	12,000	
Inventory of Supplies	8,000	
Advances for extension of a building (in anticipation of gifts and other income)	34,500	
Bonds—U.S.	40,000	$ 119,500

Student Loan Funds Assets:

Cash in Banks	$ 8,000	
Accounts Receivable	600	
Notes Receivable	81,400	
Bonds—U.S.	18,000	108,000

Endowment and Annuity Funds Assets:

Cash in Banks	$ 49,000	
Notes Receivable	1,000	
Bonds—U.S.	1,000,000	
Bonds—Other	1,500,000	
Preferred Stocks	750,000	
Common Stocks	750,000	
Real Estate Mortgages	750,000	
Contracts for Sale of Real Estate	100,000	
Real Estate	390,000	5,290,000

Educational Plant Funds Assets:

Educational Plant

Equipment	$1,250,000		
Buildings	3,500,000		
Grounds	250,000	$5,000,000	
Dormitories and other Service Properties		3,000,000	8,000,000
			$13,517,500

BALANCE SHEET—JUNE 30, 1947—*Continued*

FUNDS AND LIABILITIES

Current Funds and Liabilities:

Accounts Payable	$ 1,500		
Prepaid Tuition, etc.	10,000	$ 11,500	

Surplus

Current Balances for Designated Purposes	$ 8,000		
Undesignated	100,000	108,000	$ 119,500

Student Loan Funds:

Gifts	$ 100,000	
Reserve for Losses	8,000	108,000

Endowment and Annuity Funds:

Endowment Funds

For Current Expenses

Unrestricted	1,000,000*	
Designated	1,000,000*	

For Annual Additions to Permanent Equipment 1,500,000

For Scholarships 1,500,000 5,000,000

Annuity Funds

Actuarial Liability on Annuity Contracts	150,000	
Net Equity in Annuity Gifts .	100,000	250,000
Reserve for Losses		40,000 5,290,000

Educational Plant Funds:

Gifts

For Educational Plant	4,500,000	
For Dormitories and Other Service Properties	3,000,000*	7,500,000
Other Plant Income		500,000 8,000,000

$13,517,500

* In addition to the income from unrestricted and designated endowment funds for educational current expenses will be the income, to be used for this purpose, from $3,000,000 invested in dormitories and other income-producing properties, thus making available for the educational budget the income from $5,000,000.

directly for the building with no thought of income for the educational budget. In the latter case the gift functions as a kind of scholarship fund with benefits to all students, regardless of financial needs, in the form of providing board and room for less than cost—made possible by money which might have been used to strengthen the educational work of the college.

If a college decides not to use gifts for dormitories, etc. (except as investments), and to make such properties self-supporting, then the problem of providing its students with all needed housing and dining facilities becomes one of arranging for the necessary financing. Many institutions borrow outside money for this purpose either directly or through an affiliated corporation. We do not recommend this plan although if money for such construction can be borrowed at rates substantially lower than what the institution can make on its own endowment investments there would be that argument in its favor. This is not likely to be the case. Many institutions have paid much higher rates on such outside borrowings than they have been able to make on their own funds and in addition have carried the risk of capital losses on their outside investments.

If a college with a policy of using all gifts for strictly educational purposes needs a dormitory, it might well try to interest one or more of its friends in giving the required amount for endowment with the understanding that it be used for the construction of the dormitory as an investment with the net income designated for some purpose within the educational budget. If no such gifts are available and it is decided to finance the building with borrowed money, it is more conservative to borrow from the institution's endowment funds than from outside sources. In the former case there is only one risk—that of making the dormitory pay a net income on the amount invested; in the latter case this risk remains the same, and in addition there is the problem of finding an outside investment for the amount involved with attendant risk of capital losses.

4. College Hospital. This service should be organized on the same plan used for dormitories. A separate fee should be charged to make it self-supporting, including interest on the amount invested and provision for its retirement. The Health Service is regarded as part of the regular educational work of the college and is included in the educational budget without extra fees.

The third section of the current budget includes those operations which are regularly or occasionally necessary but which are not educational or even quasi-educational in nature. Among these activities the most frequent are the following:

1. Retiring Allowances (as distinguished from current payments to active employees to help provide future pensions). These should not be included in the current educational budget. It is assumed that such allowances have been provided for by previous premium payments. In cases where this has not been done, additional income will have to be secured for this purpose.

2. Scholarships and Grants-in-aid awarded on the basis of need. Here the institution simply takes the place of the parent in providing financial assistance to the student. (It is assumed that the full amount of tuition for every student will be accounted for and that there will be no "rebates" of tuition.) Special endowment funds provide the necessary income for scholarships.

Prizes and prize-scholarships, offered to students on the basis of their scholastic work regardless of financial need, are educational devices intended to improve the quality of the student's work and, for that reason, are included under expense for instruction.

3. Student Loans. It is assumed that interest on student loans will cover the cost of administration and losses.

4. Publicity and Alumni Bureau. It seems obvious that the cost of financial campaigns and expenses in connection with

keeping the public and the alumni interested (alumni secretary, alumni bulletin, etc.) should not be charged to the current educational budget. The item of direct advertising and other expenses in connection with annual efforts to interest students in attending college seem more doubtful. In view of the fact that some colleges are obliged to spend a great deal more money in securing the enrollment they desire than others are obliged to do, and having in mind that this expenditure in no way enhances the educational offerings of any college, it seems desirable to exclude these expenses also from the regular educational current budget.

No provision is made for any of these expenses in the proposed educational budget. The necessary income may well be provided for by annual appeals for small gifts from alumni and others.

5. Interest on Indebtedness. Interest payments, no matter for what purpose the money is borrowed, should not be included in the current educational budget. No provision has been made for such expense except in connection with the proposed $100,000 for current working capital.

The Balance Sheet presented on pages 142 and 143 is in the form recommended by the National Committee on Standard Reports for Institutions of Higher Education. The arrangement of the different sections and of the items in each section is in the order of the liquidity of assets—the more liquid being placed first. The publications of this committee and of the continued Financial Advisory Service maintained for several years by the American Council on Education are strongly recommended to the presidents, financial officers, and trustees of all colleges.

The use of the recommended forms not only will provide a valuable record year after year of an institution's financial processes, but will greatly facilitate comparative educational studies and will in time lead to a more ready public understanding of college finances. Every college should print an annual financial statement setting forth in detail its financial assets and liabilities and an operating statement with supporting details. Full publicity regarding the financial condition of a college at the end of each fiscal year will do much to develop interest in its work and to create confidence in its management.

CHAPTER XIII

Sources of Financial Support

Different types of educational institutions are needed in the United States if we are to preserve the distinctive features of our manner of life—publicly and privately supported universities, separately organized colleges, junior colleges, teachers' colleges, engineering and agricultural colleges, etc. All these various types of institutions can be carried on successfully if they can attract a satisfactory number of students and secure adequate financial support. Granted these two conditions, each type of institution will continue to carry on its work in its own way and altogether they will strengthen and enrich the life of our country more effectively than could be done by any system of uniform and controlled education. However, these two conditions of student enrollment and financial support represent quite different problems for different types of institutions, and the institutions themselves vary greatly in their ability to deal with these problems.

The future of tax-supported institutions is secure: they will be given more and more adequate financial support. If the needs of the public could be fully met by this type of institution, the path for the future would be clear. However, these institutions carry on their work under serious limitations—the menace of political control, a tendency to undue standardization of educational processes, relative lack of freedom for educational experimentation, difficulty in limiting student enrollment and scope of work, legal restrictions on religious instruction, political expediency affecting instruction in other fields, etc. Tax-supported institutions are greatly influenced by private institutions, and their path is made easier by the influence that private institutions have on the attitude of the public toward education and its ideals and methods.

Nowhere else in our nation do two institutions "in the same business" exist side by side in harmony and comparable prosperity with such an enormous price differential as there is between the endowed and the tax-supported colleges. Even the private and city hospitals are not comparable, for many city hospitals will not accept patients who are able to pay their way. The enrollments in the two types of institutions are about equal. For the year ending June 30, 1942 (the last normal year before the colleges became engaged in war training programs), the expenditures of tax-supported colleges, universities, and professional schools amounted to $283,251,646 and to $290,-811,601 for the corresponding private institutions. (*Statistical Summary of Education*, U.S. Office of Education.)

Probably no other item of public policy is more important for the future of our American way of living than to maintain our system of dual support and control for higher education—public institutions, supported by taxes and controlled basically by those who control the taxes, and private institutions, supported by gifts from many sources and controlled more largely by their own officers and immediate constituency. If there were no private institutions and higher education were supported entirely by the state, it would soon be brought under the control of those in political authority and would in time become propaganda rather than education.

On the other hand, if higher education were carried on exclusively by private institutions, its opportunities would tend to become limited to children of privileged homes. These two types of institutions are a help to each other and together provide a system which keeps educational opportunities open on a democratic basis and at the same time gives wide freedom to individual members of faculties and student bodies to pursue their studies without interference.

The most difficult problem in connection with the future of higher education in this country is that of securing adequate financial support for private colleges and universities. The future of private institutions will not depend upon how well they may have done their work in the past nor upon how great a need they may have met. It will depend entirely upon whether or not they can find adequate financial support for their work. If the private institutions could be put in a position where they could offer their opportunities to students for as low fees as state and municipal institutions charge, there would be no question about their future enrollments. This is not likely to happen, nor is it a necessary condition for their future success.

The fact that privately supported colleges have been successful in maintaining their enrollments in the face of wide differences in tuition charges indicates that many young people and their parents prefer the type of education that private support makes possible. The charges for tuition could probably be increased in most colleges. Fifteen years ago Dr. Trevor Arnett, at that time president of the General Education Board in New York, favored a policy of making the charge for tuition equal to the cost of providing the educational opportunities offered, exclusive of the original cost of educational buildings and equipment. In other words, Dr. Arnett felt that the public should provide the educational plant without cost to the student, but that the cost of maintaining the plant and providing salaries for teachers and all other current expenses should be paid by the students.

On this plan the income from endowment funds would be available for providing scholarships for students not able to pay the regular charges and for such other purposes as giving special salaries to teachers of unusual distinction and providing opportunities for such special investigation and research as would in the long run improve the quality of teaching.

It should, of course, be pointed out that colleges in the Middle West find themselves in a very different situation from those located in the East. Western colleges do their work under the shadow of great state universities where tuition even for out-of-state students is low, most of the cost being provided at public expense through taxes. In the East, colleges of liberal arts are in a region where state institutions are comparatively unimportant and where the fees charged by the great private universities are usually larger than those charged by the colleges.

It would obviously be more difficult for colleges in the Middle West to adopt Dr. Arnett's plan than for those in the East. However, the fact that colleges in the Middle West have been so successful in maintaining their enrollments, notwithstanding the much lower tuition fees in state institutions, seems to indicate that the preference shown by so many for private institutions would probably make them willing to pay still higher fees if the quality of instruction offered should seem to them to warrant the additional expense.

However, this possibility does not offer a complete solution of the financial problems of a college. Notwithstanding the present low rates of interest, an adequate endowment is still the rock on which the structure of a private college should rest. Nor has the time entirely passed for securing endowments. Many people of moderate wealth are in a position to create lasting memorials if such opportunities are effectively presented to them. Individuals should find a special appeal in the establishment of memorials to relatives, friends, or themselves. "I have built a monument to myself," said the poet Horace, "which will outlast marble and the ravages of time."

This is true of the man or woman who endows a college professorship; for $100,000 to $200,000 a professorial chair can be named in perpetuity as a memorial. Almost every college has some endowed chairs; at Knox, ten of the thirty professional chairs are endowed and named in honor of the donors. The Philip Sidney Post Professorship of Economics and the Clara A. Abbott Professorship of Biology give stability and continuity to instruction in these fields. Larger gifts for instructional purposes can be used to establish foundations, such as the Frank B. Kellogg Foundation in International Relations at Carleton; this fund of $500,000 supports several faculty members and special lecturers and provides equipment and other facilities and opportunities which would not ordinarily be available.

Buildings constitute memorials cherished by many, and it is a rare college which does not need some new building. It is a wise policy, however, to set aside part of the gift for a building to cover the added cost of maintenance; otherwise the addition of new buildings may increase the cost of upkeep to such a point that it will be necessary to reduce instructional salaries.

Not every individual donor, however, is able to give a sum large enough to erect a building or endow a professorship. Smaller amounts are sufficient to establish memorial scholarships, loan funds, or funds for prizes. The memorial gifts most helpful from the point of view of the administrator are those for undesignated endowment, in which the income is not tied to any specific use but is available for the total program of the institution. Over a period of many years changes may be so great that funds given for a too-specific purpose may be rendered useless by the disappearance of the purpose itself. Trustees should always be empowered by the donor to effect such changes in the use of gifts as time may require.

Many friends of the colleges might be willing to make substantial gifts if they understood that this could be done without reducing their income during their lifetime. The "annuity plan" makes this possible and, because of federal and in some cases state income tax exemptions, the current income of such donors might be substantially increased. They are also freed from the necessity and risks of investing their own funds. From the college point of view it is important that no obligations to pay guaranteed amounts be assumed in connection with gifts other than cash until such time as they are actually converted into cash. The net income from properties, perhaps with a reasonable charge for management deducted, may properly be paid to the annuitant, but there can be no guarantee without risk of loss to other funds of the college—a risk which should not be assumed.

When such properties are turned into cash and a definite income is guaranteed, a prudent policy limits the annuity payment to the average rate which an institution for a period of years has been able to make on its own invested funds. By following this policy the principal of the annuity gift will be preserved for the use of the college when the annuity contract expires. In exceptional cases where more than the current rate of earning is paid, the difference should be deducted from the principle of the gift, thus avoiding the necessity of making up the difference by using other funds.

The individuals who will support a college may be found in many places but they should be most numerous among the alumni and former students. Depending upon this natural loyalty, many colleges have established alumni funds with a program of annual giving from a large group for current expenses. Yale, Harvard, Cornell, Dartmouth, Amherst, and others have found this a tremendous help, resulting in $100,000 or more each year for current use. It is highly desirable to widen the basis of support. A college with a thousand alumni who contribute an individual average of $25 each year is more secure than one which depends upon five donors to give $5,000 apiece. It is also to be expected that alumni, having given small amounts to the fund during their early years, will increase their aid as time goes on and in later life will perhaps wish to perpetuate that help through a bequest.

Another steady and permanent source of income for colleges

should be the churches. The relations between the colleges and the churches during the past fifty years have not been as strong relatively as they were in the early years. This has been due partly to the fact that the colleges were able more rapidly than the churches to adjust themselves to the findings of modern science. For a time it seemed as if there was a conflict between science and religion, and this misunderstanding unquestionably tempered the zeal of many religious groups for the support of their colleges. Fortunately, this misunderstanding is gradually clearing up. The churches are beginning to take a fresh interest in their colleges, and the colleges in turn are seeing more clearly than ever before that the spirit and ideals of the churches are the only hope for a better world.

This renewed interest and growing feeling of responsibility on the part of many denominations is most encouraging. However, most of them have no national policy with reference to the development of their colleges and no adequate program for their maintenance and support. They are only beginning to realize the enormous financial responsibilities involved in maintaining institutions of higher learning. It is doubtful whether there is a Protestant denomination in America, excepting perhaps a few which have done little in the college field, that is able to maintain and properly develop the institutions for which it is now responsible.

Some of these colleges will surely die; others will be merged, and it is to be hoped that the method of denominational co-operation will prove to be the wise and practical solution of the problem in many other cases. There are in America today many great areas unprovided with adequate college opportunities for their young people. If the denominations, instead of splitting up their efforts among a number of weak and ineffective institutions, would co-operate with each other in a given region, there could be developed important regional opportunities for high-grade college instruction under Christian auspices which are likely to be realized in no other way.

If the promotion of colleges under church auspices is to be permanently effective, it would seem desirable that each denomination should have a department organized especially to assist its colleges in presenting their needs and opportunities to its members. Some churches will make contributions to support the College Department of Religion; others realize that it is equally important to have other subjects taught by men who are selected because of their understanding of and sympathy with religious values; some will establish funds to help students from a given church to attend college; others will establish these scholarships in the colleges themselves. Whatever the method, the churches should plan increasing financial help for their colleges; the mere recognition of historical relationship is not enough. Practical programs of mutual helpfulness should result in increased members and leaders for the churches, as well as financial support for the colleges.

The greatest encouragement the colleges received during the first thirty years of the present century was given by several sympathetic foundations with large endowments, notably the General Education Board, the Carnegie Foundation, and the Carnegie Corporation. To this group have been added more recently the Commonwealth Fund, the Hayden Foundation, the Rosenwald Fund, the Sloan Foundation, the Kresge Foundation, the Ford Foundation, and others, all having education as one of their chief concerns.

Dr. Walter A. Jessup, late president of the Carnegie Corporation, in his final (1944) report stated that in the thirty years since the corporation was established the budgets of higher education have grown tenfold while the income of the foundation has been diminished, so that whereas in 1911 the ratio of Carnegie aid to total higher educational income was 1 to 15, by 1940 it was 1 to 140. From this he concluded that the foundations in the future could have only a small part in the financial development of institutions and should, therefore, give their support to specific projects or organizations serving education as a whole.

The financial condition of the smaller colleges of America, however, has by no means improved as greatly since 1911 as that of the large universities. From the point of view of the colleges, the discouraging fact is that a disproportionate share of the money appropriated by foundations under their changed policies has been given to the larger and stronger institutions. The amount of aid given by the foundations in earlier years to the smaller colleges could, if judiciously allocated, be of quite as much help to these institutions under present conditions as it ever was in the past. If foundations would set aside a certain portion of their annual income for institutions of the college type and such funds were offered on conditions requiring the co-operation of other friends of these institutions, the results could be quite as significant as those achieved in earlier years.

For example, a foundation could select a group of colleges and make a conditional gift of $50,000 or more toward the endowment of a professorship, on condition that each college secure gifts of an equal or larger amount for the same purpose from not less than 250 individuals, of whom at least 50 per cent must be graduates or former students of the institution, no single gift to be more than $5,000. This endowed professorship would set a standard of salary to which other faculty salaries might be raised, and a group of such professorships would do much to lift college salaries to the level of those paid in corresponding departments of universities. It is not to be expected that gifted and well-trained teachers will be willing to continue indefinitely to work in colleges of liberal arts at salaries much lower than are available in other types of institutions.

Under modern conditions the quality of unselfishness is not closely related to the salary a man is willing to accept; but the quality of teaching in any institution is likely to be closely related to the scale of salaries it is able to pay. Such a plan of endowed professorships in a group of colleges would also enable foundations to promote instruction in certain fields needing development, such as international relations, American history and ideals, geography, music appreciation, etc. The possession of such a foundation professorship by a college would be a mark of distinction, and in securing the needed endowment under the conditions suggested many new friends would have been found. A foundation willing to undertake such a program might well develop a group of a hundred or more colleges whose increased strength and influence in the future would be due in large part to the encouragement and help thus made available.

In addition to these three groups—the alumni, the churches, and the foundations—the general public must be brought to a clearer understanding of the importance and needs of colleges of liberal arts, and to an understanding also of the necessity of giving, if we are to maintain our American form of government and our American way of life. It is often said that the American people are the most generous people in the world. This is probably true, but attention should also be called to the fact that we must be, if we wish to maintain our form of democracy.

American democracy represents a balance between too much and too little government. This balance can be preserved only if we continue to maintain a balance between total giving and total taxes—local, state, and national—for current purposes, excepting only taxes for national defense, including the cost of wars. Our distinctly American way of living is inextricably bound up with our system of dual support and control of our agencies of education, health and recreation, charities and social welfare—approximately half, until recently, supported and controlled privately and the other half through public funds.

That some of our agencies for public welfare and relief, for health and education, for recreation and leisure-time pursuits, must be supported and administered by government goes without saying. If all these agencies were dependent upon the voluntary support of citizens, many of them would languish and fail of their purpose. This is true for the simple reason that many citizens, if left entirely free, would not do their share. Some would do nothing. There are people who are not worthy of living in a democratic society. They respond only to coercion and force. If all people were of this sort, nothing but a totalitarian type of society would be practicable.

Fortunately, most people are not of this sort: along with some selfishness, there is much unselfishness; along with complacency, indifference, and neglect on the part of some, there may be found deep concern with the problems of human betterment on the part of many, and spiritual passion for the welfare of others on the part of at least a few. Such people are the hope of the world. They make possible the continuance of a democratic way of life.

The only alternative to widespread and systematic giving is some form of socialism—the ordering of men's lives by police power and the financing of their common needs by enforced taxes. It is a choice between socialism and socialized individuals. The basic objection to socialism is that in the last analysis it is founded on force; it deprives individuals of freedom, which is the first circumstance necessary for the attainment of the real ends of human existence. Even when those in power are benevolent and attempt to use their power for the public good, socialistic government means that people are compelled by force to do what they should be taught and persuaded to do by education, by the right kind of religion, and by other social influences not involving force.

Giving should not depend upon the impulse of the moment. It should be the expression of a definitely formulated purpose and of a life commitment to do one's share willingly and gladly in maintaining the organizations and agencies necessary for our common life. This is largely a matter of education. The public must be taught to understand that a willigness to share represents the spirit of a true life for the individual and is the essence of right relations with his fellows. This has been from the beginning one of the central teachings of a Christian religion and in one form or another has been at the heart of all the other great systems of religious teaching. Such a philosophy holds out the greatest hope for the future of all mankind. To understand its implications and to trust the ideas upon which it rests is to understand the meaning of democracy and to have faith in its future.

This philosophy of democracy must be accepted by corporations and other legal, commercial, and financial units as well as by individuals if the desired purposes are to be accomplished. Corporations almost without exception until a few years ago have sought to avoid making any gifts of importance. A common excuse has been that the officers of a corporation cannot give away their stockholders' money. Sometimes it is insisted that such gifts cannot be made legally. The fundamental difficulty has been that stockholders and officials of corporations have not realized the importance of giving if we are to retain our form of society. If, under the laws of any state, corporations may not make gifts, those laws should be changed. If the stockholders of a particular corporation actually control its policies, their consent and authority should be secured for a program of reasonable giving by that corporation.

It will be impossible to restore and to maintain the giving of this country on anything like a basis of equality with taxation unless corporations voluntarily take part in giving as they are compelled to take part in our system of taxation. Wherever there is a unit that can be taxed, that unit, as such, should be a source of gifts. Fortunately, corporations are beginning to see more clearly than ever before the necessity for giving if we are to avoid still further concentration of power in government. They are beginning to realize that systematic giving and private enterprise go hand in hand; that taxation and government control are inevitable companions. Their changing attitude constitutes the greatest single hope of our being able to maintain the balance between public and private agencies necessary to our form of democracy.

If the American public, including corporations, can be educated and persuaded to maintain a system of gifts adequate to the needs of our democracy, there is no question that the colleges will be given their share. A heavy burden of responsibility rests upon the trustees and presidents of these institutions to see that widespread programs of public education and persuasion regarding the necessity of gifts in a democracy are effectively carried on.

If it is in the interests of the public that individuals and corporations should give generously, this fact should receive much greater recognition in the tax policies of our federal government than is being given at the present time. Democracy will continue only so long as it succeeds in keeping in places of public authority and responsibility people who really believe in its principles and methods. Those responsible for administering the affairs of the federal government at the present time must decide whether they wish to retain our American system of divided support and control of education, public health, welfare, etc., or whether they believe it would be better to look forward to a policy of having these public services entirely supported and controlled by the government. Whatever policy is adopted in regard to taxation should be determined only after careful consideration of the whole situation that is likely to develop as a result of that policy. It would be shortsighted merely to seek income for the government regardless of the long-reaching effects of such a decision.

If it is desirable to maintain the balance between public and private agencies as we have contended, it would seem to us wise for the federal government to offer complete exemption from inheritance taxes for gifts for public purposes, such as education, health, welfare, etc., and to increase the income tax exemption from the present 15 per cent to 50 per cent for individuals, and from 5 per cent to 15 per cent for corporations. Such increases in federal tax exemptions for individuals and corporations would probably do more than could be accomplished in any other way to induce them to increase their gifts. The future of privately supported colleges, like the future of all religious and charitable organizations which derive their support from gifts, will depend to a large extent upon the tax policies of the federal government.

A college, through its president and trustees, must engage in a continuous campaign for financial support, with occasional special efforts for specific objectives or at strategic times such as anniversaries or the death of some outstanding person connected with the college. In this perpetual effort great assistance can be given by alumni and friends, particularly if they are lawyers advising clients on tax matters or bequests in their wills, or bankers administering estates, or corporation officials deciding the policies and budgets of large organizations. The financial future of American higher education must not rest entirely upon the shoulders of college executives; it is a responsibility which must be shared by every citizen who believes in a free democratic form of society and the educational institutions that will help to keep our country free.

CHAPTER XIV

Education and Government

The social controls that have recently been developing on every hand in America are hailed as something new under the sun, and therefore better than what we have had before. But the controls are old—as old as government itself—the only new feature is the form of government that is pressing them upon the people. In the past it was tyranny or monarchy or oligarchy that forced individuals into patterns under a theory of the divine right of kings. But the American republic was formed on a new basis, which repudiated the theories and practices of the past. It was unique in that it was established by free men.

They did not acknowledge government as the source of their rights as citizens, but insisted that as individuals they possessed all the rights a human being can have. These rights are an essential part of what it means to be a person; they are inherent in personality and derive from the inner nature of the universe itself—that is, from God. The phraseology of the Declaration of Independence is definite: "all men . . . are endowed by their Creator with certain unalienable rights." It is perfectly clear from the context of history, both before and after the Revolution, that they regarded liberty as the greatest of these rights.

The purpose of the Constitution of the United States was not to convey rights to individual citizens, but to specify the limits imposed by citizens upon the government. Our forefathers, desiring their freedom above all else and having thrown off the shackles of the government under which they had previously lived, did not propose to permit any new government to usurp such authority as would interfere with their personal lives as free men. On the other hand, they recognized the necessity of conducting together certain matters which concerned their common life; for this purpose they established an agency of their common will to which they delegated certain police powers and limited powers to tax.

They realized that they were dealing with powers which might destroy what they cherished most. They were under no illusions as to the real nature of government. In the words of Washington, "Government is not reason, it is not eloquence— it is force! Like fire, it is a dangerous servant and a fearful master." They moved so cautiously that the central government which they first constructed was not strong enough to accomplish the purposes for which it was intended. The Confederation did not have power enough. It was necessary to go a step or two further, but they were determined not to take too many steps. The Constitution was an expression of this necessity and of this determination.

After the Constitution had been formulated, some contended that nothing more was needed; others, especially Jefferson, who was in Europe when the Constitution was planned, insisted that the specific rights of individuals which were implied in the Constitution should be more explicitly stated; therefore, a "Bill of Rights" consisting of the first ten Amendments was immediately added. The Tenth Amendment reads: "The powers not delegated to the United States by the Constitution, nor prohibited by it to the States, are reserved to the States, respectively, or to the people." It is difficult to see how human ingenuity could have devised a more effective instrument for safeguarding the rights and freedom of sovereign citizens.

The problem of steering a middle course between too much and too little government was a difficult one for them, as it has been in the changing circumstances of every succeeding generation, and as it is today in the field of international relations. However, their problem was made easier and the outcome more enduring because they had a single guiding principle. That principle was freedom. They were not aiming primarily at efficiency in government, nor at social security, nor even at social justice, desirable as all these things were in their day as in ours. Their purpose was to establish a society in which men might be free.

In 1788 Patrick Henry, in a speech in the Virginia Convention called to ratify the Constitution, said, "The first thing I have at heart is American liberty; the second thing is American Union." By 1830 Webster realized that mere sentiment is not enough and that liberty will never last long without effective and authoritative government. He referred to "liberty first and union afterward" as "words of delusion and folly" and closed his great speech in reply to Hayne with the words "liberty and union, now and forever, one and inseparable." Lincoln saw even more clearly that liberty and freedom can never be the permanent possession of any people without the right kind of government, and his devotion to the Union sprang from his conviction that it represented mankind's best hope for freedom—"that we here highly resolve that these dead shall not have died in vain—that this nation, under God, shall have a new birth of freedom."

For more than a century and a half our Constitution has served as the basis for a way of life which has brought to the rank and file of our people as individuals a sense of dignity and personal worth equaled under no other system of social or political thought. As a by-product of the spiritual ideals to which we have thus been committed, the citizens of the United States have enjoyed a standard of material conveniences and comforts and a level of cultural and educational opportunities achieved in no other country. All the progress we have made so far as a nation, all our institutions, all the blessings, both material and spiritual, which our citizens have enjoyed have resulted from a social and political philosophy based on the assumption that man is a spiritual being—that men and women as individuals possess in themselves all rights, and that the primary function of government is to safeguard these individual rights and to reconcile them when they come into conflict. The state itself has no rights or functions of its own. It is merely an instrumentality of the will of the people and has no authority except such authority as may be delegated to it by sovereign citizens.

The Old World concept of the state (often identified in the public mind with the crown or royal family) as having inherent rights and functions of its own has been chiefly responsible for the miseries of mankind. It has been the archenemy of men and women as individuals. Too much government, regardless of the theory on which it is based, is mankind's worst foe. By government in this connection is meant two definite and specific things, and only these two—police power (the right to use force) and power to levy taxes.

There are many ways in which the machinery of modern government can be used to advantage where authority and coercion are not involved, nor appropriations requiring taxes: for example, personal conferences between government officials and civilian leaders in a spirit of co-operation in common tasks, national and regional conferences resulting in suggested plans and procedures, national surveys, public discussions in the press and radio, and in many other ways. The leadership of our State Department in the field of cultural relations with Latin America is a good example of such a possibility involving the co-operation of individuals, colleges and universities, and private organizations like the Institute of International Education, each free to make its own contribution.

The founders of our country had fought for their freedom and they proposed to keep it. They were determined to avoid building up a government which would make it impossible for them and their posterity to live in the enjoyment of the freedom they had won and of the rights they had established. To this end they ordained that the federal government should have no part in education. This was a matter to be left entirely to the states and more particularly to the local communities. Our Federal Constitution says nothing about education. This was not an oversight. It was a deliberate omission after discussion in the Convention. The founders of our government, many of them college graduates and professional men, were deeply interested in education and saw clearly its relation to the future of any society.

Their purpose was to develop a certain type of society, a society based on the assumption that freedom is the first condition of all worth-while existence and that the ends of human life can never be realized under the coercions of government. Upon this basis was built the first truly democratic system of education in the world, a system free from domination by the central government, with local school boards and independent colleges. Later, when the first state universities were chartered, they were given grants of land as endowment, so that they might remain as free as possible from the political pressures of even their own state governments. This localization of the controls of education still remains the greatest safeguard of our freedom and the surest guarantee that no dictatorship will ever take root among us.

The problem of maintaining this independence in education is primarily a question of financial support. As we have indicated in the preceding chapter, the solution of this problem is directly related to the tax policies of the federal government. Many years ago Chief Justice Marshall pointed out a possibility which has today become a menace, when he said, "The power to tax is the power to destroy." In 1913 the citizens of the United States, probably without fully realizing the implications of what they were doing, gave the federal government, through the Sixteenth Amendment to the Constitution, practically unlimited power to tax the incomes of all citizens.

The possibilities thus created of a vast federal income began to stimulate fantastic dreams of what might be accomplished for the material welfare of the people through the agency of the federal government. For twenty years only cautious steps were taken in the direction of these dreams. With the beginning of the Franklin D. Roosevelt administration, however, a new era was launched in the history of the American people. Whole sections of our population have been encouraged to expect from government a type of material benefit which can never be had from our form of government either now or in the years to come. If such programs are forced through by political propaganda, they will bring with them profound changes in the structure of our government and ultimately our whole social and political philosophy will be changed. Our American way of life will then be ended and freedom will be scorned.

Some of our political leaders in recent years seem to believe that we should have a better country if this happened. In a speech in New York in February, 1934, a then member of the Cabinet said that "a bloodless political and social revolution occurred on Election Day, 1932" and that "for the first time in history the Government of the United States had assumed responsibility for the well-being of all the people." Without any change in the Constitution, other than the power to tax incomes conferred by the Sixteenth Amendment, the whole structure of our government has been changed, at least temporarily, and our distinctively American social and political concepts are being replaced by others which have been regarded until recently as incompatible with our form of government and our American way of life.

The discussion of this problem should be completely disentangled from problems relating to the war. War cannot be conducted on the basis of democratic principles. Every democracy must temporarily give up its basic philosophy in order to carry on war successfully. War demands the gathering up of all power by the central government and the yielding by every citizen of all his rights, including life itself, if necessary. The strongest argument against war as a method of settling international disputes is the unavoidable necessity that these things must be done. But it would be a poor reward for all our sacrifices if we should lose the things we fought for as a result of our efforts to defend them.

It is possible that a majority of voters could be secured in support of totally confiscatory taxation—more likely to happen if the central government controlled the agencies of education —but if that should ever occur the majority would have voted the end of the American republic. Until recently it did not seem possible that such a condition could develop, but in recent years the federal government has so expanded itself, has assumed so many functions constitutionally reserved to the people, and has responded so readily to the propaganda pressures of special interest groups seeking federal benefits that Lincoln's "of the people, by the people, and for the people" seems to be giving way to the idea of government in its own right. The instrument of the people thus looms as a Frankenstein monster which could destroy its creator by confiscating his means of support.

President Coolidge stated: "I do not believe that the government should seek social legislation in the guise of taxation. If we are to adopt socialism, it should be presented to the people of this country as socialism and not under the guise of a law to collect revenue." Has our national destiny run its cycle? Has democracy failed, and are we to return without a struggle to the stateism of the Roman emperors, Louis XIV, Czar Nicholas, and Bismarck? Was the vision of Jefferson a delusion, that we should now reject it for the leviathan state? Is the all-encompassing state the apex of human development? We have been assured that it is by foreign propagandists; will they poison our hearts against our own ideals?

Our federal government has grown so mighty with war powers that it will not be easy to deprive it of these powers when the circumstances that justified them have passed. There is no area in which it is more important that this be done than in education. American colleges and universities were eager and sincere in their desire to make the largest possible contribution to the war effort. Their personnel and equipment were placed at the service of the government. They became instruments of the government for the training of members of the armed forces and for the solution of scientific problems that led straight to the winning of the war. It would be an easy matter for the colleges to depend upon the government for continued support, but their freedom would be lost if this became a permanent policy.

The freedom of education is the precondition of all other freedoms. First among the rights of a free people is the right to think. This implies their right of access to the sources of materials for thought and of training in its methods. It involves keeping the channels of public discussion wide open without direction from government. It means the right of peaceful public assembly under all circumstances. No police power should ever be used to prevent people's coming together for the discussion of problems which interest them and have to do with their welfare. It means the freedom of the press and the use of the radio without such supervision from the government as will interfere with its maintenance as a channel of unhindered expression of personal opinion.

No such freedom as this could be found in totalitarian Germany, Italy, or Japan. Sometime soon after Hitler came to power a new official was appointed in Germany with some such title as "Minister of Propaganda and Enlightenment"—a controller of the thoughts of the German people. One can scarcely imagine anything more contrary to the spirit of our country than the appointment of any such officer.

However, we are not entirely free from such possibilities. In 1918 there was submitted to Congress a bill proposing an appropriation of one hundred million dollars a year for education, to be distributed among the states upon a plan involving a dollar of state money for every federal dollar. This would have meant that a small group in Washington would control the spending of $200,000,000 a year in the field of education in this country. This was at that time about 20 per cent of our entire national budget for education. The proposal was a menace to the future of our free institutions and sooner or later would have involved dictation from Washington. The sponsors of the bill, of course, disclaimed having any such thought, but they overlooked the inescapable law that the sources of support inevitably become the sources of control.

Having this situation in mind, President Nicholas Murray Butler in his annual report for 1921 to the trustees of Columbia University made the following statement: "One of the most noteworthy of recent developments in American life is the zeal with which machinery is designed and built ostensibly to serve various public interests and undertakings, but in reality to control them. Perhaps in no other way is the decline of faith in liberty so clearly marked. . . . When anything appears to go wrong, or when any desirable movement seems to lag, a cry goes up for the creation of some new board or commission, and for an appropriation of public funds to maintain it in reasonable comfort. An infinite number of blank forms must be filled and an infinite number of records must be kept, classified and audited at steadily mounting cost. . . .

"So far as education is concerned, there has been overorganization for a long time past. Too many persons are engaged in supervising, in inspecting and in recording the work of other persons. There is too much machinery, and in consequence a steady temptation to lay more stress upon the form of education than upon its content. Statistics displace scholarship. There are, in addition, too many laws and too many precise laws, and not enough opportunity for those mistakes and failures, due to individual initiative and experiment, which are the foundation for great and lasting success.

"It is now proposed to bureaucratize and to bring into uniformity the educational system of the whole United States, while making the most solemn assurance that nothing of the kind is intended. The glory and the successes of education in the United States are due to its freedom, to its unevennesses, to its reflection of the needs and ambitions and capacities of local communities, and to its being kept in close and constant touch with the people themselves. There is not money enough in the United States, even if every dollar of it were expended on education, to produce by federal authority or through what is naïvely called co-operation between the federal government and the several states, educational results that would be at all comparable with those that have already been reached under the free and natural system that has grown up among us. . . . It is universally acknowledged that the unhappy decline in German university freedom and effectiveness, and the equally unhappy subjection of the educated classes to the dictates of the political and military ruling groups, were the direct result of the highly centralized and efficient control from Berlin of the nation's schools and universities.

"For Americans now to accept oversight and direction of their tax-supported schools and colleges from Washington would mean that they had failed to learn one of the plainest and most weighty lessons of the war. It is true that education is a national problem and a national responsibility; it is also true that it has been characteristic of the American people to solve their most difficult national problems and to bear their heaviest national responsibilities through their own action in the field of liberty, rather than through the agency of organized government. Once more to tap the federal treasury under the guise of aiding the states, and once more to establish an army of bureaucrats in Washington and another army of inspectors roaming at large throughout the land, will not only fail to accomplish any permanent improvement in the education of our people, but it will assist in effecting so great a revolution in our American form of government as one day to endanger its perpetuity. . . . The true path of advance in education is to be found in the direction of keeping the people's schools closely in touch with the people themselves. . . . Unless the school is both the work and the pride of the community which it serves, it is nothing.

"A school system that grows naturally in response to the needs and ambitions of a hundred thousand different localities, will be a better school system than any which can be imposed upon those localities by the aid of grants of public money from the federal treasury, accompanied by federal regulations, federal inspections, federal reports and federal uniformities."

Since 1918 repeated attempts have been made to persuade Congress to appropriate vast sums for the current support of education along the general lines first proposed, except that the matching feature—a state dollar to go with each federal dollar —has been dropped and repudiated as involving too obvious federal control. The case for federal aid to education has been admirably formulated and may now be regarded as having reached its final stage. It is doubtful whether any future presentation will be more convincing. The bills now submitted to Congress are based on surveys and studies conducted by competent persons who are close to the problems involved—a little too close, perhaps, for the widest perspective.

The claim that federal aid is needed rests basically on the acknowledged inequalities of educational opportunities to be found in the various states. It is pointed out that many of the poorest states have the largest percentage of children and that the percentage of tax money that goes for education is largest in some states which notwithstanding this effort are able to maintain only substandard schools. It is further pointed out that the freedom of individuals to live where they please spreads the handicaps of poor education beyond state lines and involves every state in concern for the educational facilities of every other, thus creating a truly national responsibility.

In these presentations no emphasis is placed on the fact that, in spite of the inequalities pointed out and other weaknesses in our schools, the United States through its system of decentralized control and local responsibility has developed more widespread educational opportunities and has enabled a larger percentage of its population to profit by them and at higher levels than has been possible in any large nation under any other system. Nor do the proponents of federal aid make clear that no state is devoting an impressive amount of money to education if considered as a percentage of its total income rather than of the tax dollar. If states and local school districts should become convinced that no federal funds will be available, it is not unreasonable to believe that local interest and initiative would still continue to improve their schools.

The basic argument against federal aid for schools is that it would place in the hands of those in political authority the power to transform our whole way of life. Certain controls are conceded to be necessary from the start—joint responsibility in the preparation of educational plans for each state with authority resting with the United States commissioner of education for final approval according to standards which he determines; for regional representatives of the federal agency and for financial accounting to it of all money spent, and for annual reports covering the educational results achieved. These controls involve supervision not only of funds supplied by the federal government but of state funds as well. Dr. John J. Tigert, president of the University of Florida, formerly United States Commissioner of Education, for eight years in charge of administering the funds of the federal Office of Education, has pointed out the menace inherent in all proposals for permanent federal aid to education:

"We have shown that federal aid to the schools must be attended by federal control under present conditions if we are to avoid general waste and misuse of these funds. We have also pointed out that federal control will tend to become greater and that centralized operation of the schools is a menace to our institutions and ideals. . . . If we turn over to the federal government the responsibility of the operation of our schools, we have forged the weapons whereby some able and self-seeking individual may some day transform our political, social, and economic system." In a later statement (1940) he says: "There is grave danger that somewhere along through the years, in the oft recurring crises that inevitably confront us, someone may be tempted to take up the weapons which have been forged by the entrance of our government in the field of education and use them as a way of affecting the thoughts of 20,000,000 children in the elementary schools and 6,000,000 in the high schools, with the result that a new idea of government, a new social order and a new economic order will be formed far from our present ideals."

The recent proposal of the present administration that a "universal training program" (the word "military" to be omitted) be established to give "our young people a background in the disciplinary approach of getting along with one another" and to inform them "on what this government is, what it stands for—its responsibilities"—a national program for the indoctrination of all youth by the Army—would seem to leave little to the imagination as to what would happen now if those responsible for this proposal had authority over the schools of the country.

It would be nothing short of a national calamity to have a few men in Washington given the authority, in connection with this recent proposal or any other plan, to control the thinking of the people of this country. There is no man competent to think for the United States—no three or four men competent to do so, no fifty or a hundred—no thousand or ten thousand men who should be given the right to compel their fellow citizens to follow their modes of thought or to support their conclusions. The whole idea of having a few people do the thinking and having the rest become followers and loyal subjects is repugnant to the spirit of America and contrary to its fundamental ideas. All such proposals represent theories of social control diametrically opposed to those upon which this country was founded and upon the basis of which we have made such wonderful progress in the comparatively few years of our national life.

The fundamental assumption of our government is that there is no sovereignty anywhere except the sovereignty of the individual. As Lincoln said, "No man is good enough to govern another man without that other's consent." Oswald Spengler, who profoundly disbelieves in our form of government, in his book *The Hour of Decision,* written a few years ago, says that "this whole crushing depression is purely and simply the result of the decline of State power." Much of the political machinery set up in the world in recent years is based on the same conviction—a denial of the sovereignty of the individual and the assumption that a few people have the right to use the instrumentalities of government to force their ideas upon their fellows and compel their submission. There is nothing new in these procedures. They are based on old ideas which have been repeatedly tried and have always resulted in privileges for the few and in slavery, or at least submission, for the mass of the people.

The ideas upon which this country was founded have never yet had a fair trial, so far as the world as a whole is concerned. Even in our own country their application has been limited and in part thwarted by the rapid development of our industrial life, involving constant and in many respects radical changes in social relations and in the distribution of wealth. But, in spite of all this, a life of freedom and of reasonable prosperity for the masses of our population has been achieved to a degree beyond that attained by any other nation. We shall in time see more clearly than we do now the application of our democratic principles to the industrial, financial, and social problems that confront us, and with that increased understanding will come fresh confidence in our basic conceptions and a larger life for all our people.

In the meantime, let us not seek to find a solution of the material problems that confront us by reverting to ideas which have been tried out time and again and which have resulted not in the enlargement of life but in its degradation. The ideal of individual liberty and the rights that go with it—the right to think being the most important of all—are more precious than any material advantage that could possibly be secured by their sacrifice. We must not barter our freedom for any material prosperity, nor for any easy and quick solution of the problems that trouble us today.

Thinking based on integrity and good will is our hope for the future—liberal education based on religion and made effective through democratic society. The freedoms we have cherished—intellectual and spiritual, political and economic—are an essential unity, and the understanding of this unity and of its implications for ourselves and for the world is the concern of our American colleges—for freedom.

INDEX